WHAT PEOPLE ARE SAYING ABOUT BEN MOLLIN AND DECONSTRUCTED

"*Deconstructed* is a wild ride. Ben went from being a celebrity hairdresser to completely burning his life down, then rebuilding it from scratch in Sedona. What I love about this book is how honest Ben is about the whole process—the destruction, the recovery, finding his purpose. He's not just telling his story; he's sharing what he learned so others can benefit. If you're stuck or looking to make a major change in your life, this book will give you the inspiration you need to recreate yourself."

—Scotty Kummer, Podcast Host, *Ten Junk Miles*

"This story is told with brutal honesty. It is compelling and filled with vulnerability. Each vignette is infused with raw emotion, humor, or a solid gut punch of reality. Curling up with this book is like listening to an old friend. I am convinced it will touch hearts and change lives."

—Mary Bernas

"This book is achingly human. It traces the winding path of an old punk—through phases of hair, identity, and everything in between—with stories that glitter with the grit of Bravo TV fame to the shadowy corners of mental health. Each chapter feels like a nod: *I see you.* It's a companion for anyone who's ever tried to patch themselves and their messy lives back together."

—Amanda Stump

"This is a complete story of the pursuit for success and happiness. The struggle, the top of the mountain, the fall, and the path to peaceful existence. This book took me down unexpected and familiar roads and opened my eyes to the importance of unconditional love and support for those in our orbit and how the drive for success affects those relationships. There is something for everyone here."

—Joe Venturella

"Reading Ben Mollin's book was a powerful and emotional experience for me—not just because I know him personally and lived through many of the moments he shares, but because I had no idea the depth of pain he was carrying all along. I had heard so many of his stories over the years, and they were always entertaining or inspiring. But now, seeing the raw truth and the context behind them is absolutely eye-opening.

What strikes me most is Ben's unshakable 'can do' spirit—how he's taken his struggles, processed them with honesty, and used them as fuel to do good in the world. His journey is not just about resilience, it's about transformation. This book is a testament to his heart, grit, and purpose."

—Michelle Goldstein

"*Deconstructed* is an inspiring and laughably entertaining story of perseverance and discovery. It's about analyzing what's important and ridding yourself of the unnecessary. Sandwiched in between valuable life lessons are some truly hilarious encounters that would only happen to the author. A great read for anyone who's felt completely overwhelmed by life's twists and turns."

—Evan Roberts

"Have you ever wondered about the life of your hair stylist? Me neither, until now. Ben cuts my hair. After reading this book, I will never look at him or any service provider the same way. Everyone has a story. And Ben's story took me on an unexpected life journey with important lessons."

—"a lucky client of Ben," Fran

"Ben's book is funny and full of interesting anecdotes from a life that has been anything but ordinary. More importantly, it is an inspiring testimony about facing life's hardest challenges, staring them straight in the eyes, talking directly to our negative inner voices, and taming them one day at a time, every single day. When everything seems overwhelming and hopeless, focus on the present moment right here and now and take one step at a time in the right direction. Easy to say, but Ben is proof that it does work."

—Frederico Calabrese

"Ben is a natural storyteller. His words are captivating, honest, and down to earth. He admits his 'failures,' which is too strong a word—shall we say, his 'lapses in judgment' maybe? But he doesn't let them define him. He learns from his experiences, and anyone reading his book can do the same.

I think his book is an inspiration to anyone who faces hardships and/or questions what is right for their future. If some of his experiences seem too personal to share, you shouldn't expect anyone to sugarcoat their memories. Ben is confident in his own skin and he has earned that right. I can't wait to hear Ben read this book in his own voice. It will make it that much more special."

—Wendy Lee

"Reading Ben's book might be the closest I've ever gotten to listening to punk rock music—and actually enjoying it. I've never met anyone who could reach so many people across a myriad of invisible barriers, whether that's age, gender, religion, politics, etc. Somehow, he has the ability to reach almost anyone, regardless of socio-economic status or background. No words seem adequate to relay my admiration for Ben or how inspiring his book is."

—Kathy Postma

"Ben's candid reflections on addiction, failure, and mental health are essential reading for anyone who has ever faced their own darkness. That's all of us. His story is inspiring, flawed, hilarious, painful, fearless and ultimately, deeply human.

Through it all, Ben stays true to himself: brutally honest, self-deprecating, and unwavering in his pursuit of healing and purpose.

Open your heart. Open your mind. Let this story in. By the time you turn the last page, you'll see the world—and yourself—a little differently."

—Dave Schoon, President, Midwest Refrigeration

"*Deconstructed* is a journey into journeys, travels through times within a time that as a reader you feel like you were a part of the story. You feel like a non-player character in a simulation that's replaying the moment. In doing this, without realizing it, you have been transported. You realize quickly that while you walk with the writer through these happenings that birthed lessons, you too learned from that lesson one of your own.

I've known Ben now for approaching nine years, and since the day of meeting him I've called him Yoda. I was his chauffeur from the airport to the hotel Airbnb we were renting. His seminar experience was in our itinerary and I was highly intrigued. It was a class that would forever change my life for the better. I feel like I was born for the first time that day and began living my life in the ways I was meant to. My life took off like a rocket that day and it's still in orbit. Ben changed my life, unlocked me, and helped me save myself so I could save others. He is a Jedi of self-help."

—Keon Washington

"I was ready to say no to a keynote, but hiring Ben changed everything for me. He helped me find the power, clarity, and confidence I didn't know I had. Because of him, I now own every stage I step on and inspire thousands with the voice he helped me discover."

—Mireya Villarreal, Founder & CEO, Pink Pewter

"I met Ben when he was very young and have watched him grow into a confident, knowledgeable, and innovative person. He's productive and driven, always pursuing his goals. My wife and I have always held a special place in our hearts for Ben and his entire family."

—Joe Paciorek, Owner, Planet Color

"When you first meet Ben, you'll see a punk rock/techno/hippie exterior, but if you look deeper, you'll find a gem of a soul. Ben Mollin has wildfire inside of him that fuels his passions and inspires those of us who know him. His story will resonate with those seeking something that we, in the ultrarunning community, call 'flow.' Make no assumptions about Ben. He may flow like a river, but at times, he is a tsunami."

—Oscar Delgado

"Ben Mollin is one of the most genuine people I know. Watching his evolution over the years has been nothing short of inspiring. This book captures the kind of transformation that comes from deep internal awareness, the kind that leads to real happiness and lasting impact.

I also know that if I ever needed to carry a dead weight 100 miles through the forest, Ben wouldn't just say yes. He'd lace up, pack electrolytes, and give a TED Talk on transformation halfway through. That's the kind of ride-or-die, soul-evolved ultramarathoner he is."

—Corey Gray, Podcast Host,
***Your Day Off* by Hairdustry**

"I met Ben years ago at a hair show after *Shear Genius*. We'd hang out at conventions, and I knew Ben was as fucked up as I was. He saw life through a different lens that was beyond creative—some would call extreme, but to me it was genius. We'd joke about wild scenarios like faking his death and having an epic comeback like Makaveli. I remember editing a photo of Ben on the convention floor, making it look like he was rising from the grave. People walked by like WTF??? I knew Ben was on a mission with something big.

Then he disappeared from the hair scene. Months later on social media, I see this guy, who used to be a little pudgy, running 30 miles and eating protein bars mid-run. I'm like, here this crazy bastard goes again!!! Then 30 miles became 40, then 50, then 75. His mind and willpower are unexplainable. While fake people color their hair purple and think they're unique because they're outspoken on social media, Ben actually thinks outside the norm and makes shit happen. He goes all in, balls to the wall. Now he's running over 100 miles in one shot. Like who does that?? BEN 'FN' MOLLIN does!!"

—Bradley Tuggle

DECONSTRUCTED

KILL THE THING THAT'S KILLING YOU

BEN F'N MOLLIN

with Lori Lynn

DECONSTRUCTED
Kill the Thing That's Killing You

For permission requests, speaking inquiries, and bulk order purchase options, email benmollin@gmail.com or visit benfnmollin.com.

ISBN: 979-8-9992030-1-4 (Paperback)
ISBN: 979-8-9931662-0-9 (Hardcover)
ISBN: 979-8-9931662-1-6 (eBook)

Designed by Transcendent Publishing | TranscendentPublishing.com
Co-written with and edited by Lori Lynn | LoriLynnEnterprises.com
Cover Photography by Christi Bushby

WARNING: This book contains adult language. Some material may not be suitable for sensitive readers. If you're listening to the audiobook while you're driving, don't crash your car. You will laugh, you will cry. Just try not to die. Enjoy your book.

Printed in the United States of America.

DESIDERATA

Go placidly amid the noise and the haste, and remember what peace there may be in silence. As far as possible, without surrender, be on good terms with all persons.

Speak your truth quietly and clearly; and listen to others, even to the dull and the ignorant; they too have their story.

Avoid loud and aggressive persons; they are vexatious to the spirit. If you compare yourself with others, you may become vain or bitter, for there will always be greater and lesser persons than yourself.

Enjoy your achievements as well as your plans. Keep interested in your own career, however humble; it is a real possession in the changing fortunes of time.

Exercise caution in your business affairs, for the world is full of trickery. But let this not blind you to what virtue there is; many persons strive for high ideals, and everywhere life is full of heroism.

Be yourself. Especially do not feign affection. Neither be cynical about love; for in the face of all aridity and disenchantment, it is as perennial as the grass.

Take kindly the counsel of the years, gracefully surrendering the things of youth.

Nurture strength of spirit to shield you in sudden misfortune. But do not distress yourself with dark imaginings. Many fears are born of fatigue and loneliness.

Beyond a wholesome discipline, be gentle with yourself. You are a child of the universe no less than the trees and the stars; you have a right to be here.

And whether or not it is clear to you, no doubt the universe is unfolding as it should. Therefore be at peace with God, whatever you conceive Him to be. And whatever your labors and aspirations, in the noisy confusion of life, keep peace in your soul. With all its sham, drudgery and broken dreams, it is still a beautiful world. Be cheerful. Strive to be happy.

—Max Ehrmann ©1927

CONTENTS

To my wife Angela and our son Marco.

This book is also dedicated to anyone who's ever been chopped down at the knees by life. To anyone who's ever lost their dreams and purpose. It's the sign you've been waiting for to get out of your head, off your ass, and f'n go get it.

This book is dedicated to *you*.

FOREWORD

Ben and I grew up in the same city, though he was a few years older. I first knew him through his brother in middle school—not closely, but with deep admiration.

Here was this guy who was unapologetically himself: talented, energetic, punk in the best way. He didn't give a damn what people thought, and he marched to the beat of his own drum. While I might have looked like I fit in with the jock crowd, I was drawn to his authenticity and his passion for music.

From the outside, Ben always seemed to be into something cool—whether it was his shows, his record shop, striking out as an early entrepreneur, or, later, his reality TV fame. What I didn't see, what none of us could see, was the internal struggle he was fighting.

Success can be just as dangerous as failure, and Ben's journey would take him from the heights of public recognition to the brink of suicide.

While Ben was chasing music and fame, my own path took a hard left at nineteen when I got a girl pregnant and found myself working the assembly line at the Ford Chicago plant in the trim department. Surrounded by coworkers counting down their thirty years to pension, I knew I needed a way out.

So I enrolled in college and brought textbooks to work. Between installing seatbelts and B-pillars on those slow-rolling 1998 Ford Taurus automobiles, I'd steal fifteen seconds here and there to read. Eight to ten hours a day, five days a week, for five years. That's how I graduated magna cum laude—fifteen seconds at a time.

That Ford plant taught me something crucial: no one cares about your circumstances. No one's waiting to rescue you. Your parents care, but the world doesn't owe you anything. You're not entitled to success just because you think you deserve it. These might sound like harsh words, but they're liberating ones. They mean you have the power to change your story.

After Ford, those stolen seconds of learning led me to build two of the fastest-growing companies in the United States: Launch Digital Marketing and Dealer Inspire. I sold both companies for over $200 million, achieving everything I'd dreamed of during those brief reading breaks on the factory floor.

But success felt hollow.

I had everything I'd worked for and felt empty anyway. I was unhealthy, caught up in bad habits and a hectic lifestyle. When I finally looked in the mirror and took honest stock of where I was physically and mentally, I realized alcohol was one of the culprits. My father had died from alcoholism, and my younger brother was spending his weekends trying to sober up. I was headed down the same path.

During COVID, my wife and I quit alcohol for 75 days. For the first time in decades, I felt amazing. But those cravings were still there, so I found a substitute: non-alcoholic beer. That discovery led me to create Go Brewing, a company built around the idea that better choices lead to better lives.

It was during this wellness journey that Ben and I reconnected. I started seeing his posts about ultramarathons just as I was getting into endurance sports myself. Here we were—two guys from Calumet City, the same small town that most people don't escape from, on a personal-transformation quest through extreme physical challenges.

When I had Ben on my podcast *Not Almost There*, I was blown away by his story.

The struggles I couldn't see from the outside, the battles he was fighting while appearing to have it all together—even during his reality TV days. His phrase "I'm just going to burn it all down and start over" became the name of one of our beers.

You can still find "Burn It Down" IPA on Amazon, our website (gobrewing.com), and even in some stores—scan the QR code and it takes you to Ben's story. Because sometimes that's exactly what you need to do: burn down the life that's killing you to build one worth living.

Fate had one more twist in store. On our opening weekend of creating one of the first better-for-you non-alcoholic taprooms in the country, I had arranged for James Lawrence, the Iron Cowboy, to speak and join us for a workout. This same athlete's documentary had earlier become a lifeline for Ben during his darkest moments. Sometimes the universe has a sense of timing that defies explanation.

What you'll find in Ben's book isn't just another transformation story—it's a raw, unflinching journey from reality TV fame to the brink of suicide, and ultimately to rebirth as an ultra-endurance athlete and suicide prevention advocate. It's a manual for anyone who feels trapped by their circumstances, their genetics, their past, or their fears.

Ben's journey from the depths of his struggle to becoming someone who inspires others through ultramarathons and honest storytelling proves that transformation is possible. But it requires something most people aren't willing to muster: the courage to tear down everything that isn't serving you and start over.

This book will challenge you, inspire you, and maybe even save your life. Ben's wit cuts through the darkness, his vulnerability hits you in the gut, and his resilience will leave you questioning what you're truly capable of. Because sometimes the most powerful thing you can do is kill the thing that's killing you—before it kills you first.

If you've ever felt trapped by your own success or wondered if there's more to life than what you've built, this book isn't just recommended reading—it's required.

—Joe Chura
Serial Entrepreneur
Founder of Go Brewing
Podcast Host of *Not Almost There*

THE STARTING LINE

**"We are all born the same.
We all die the same.
Some choose good.
Some choose evil.
We are all children of God."**

—Mary Ann Marshall,
age 92, Ben's oldest living client

The End (Almost)

The first time I tried to kill myself, I was about to turn 14.

My parents told me I had a rare blood disorder and would need to wear a helmet when I started my freshman year of high school.

I stood there thinking, *No sports? I can't run? You want me to just sit around with an f'n helmet on? There's no way I'm gonna be "helmet boy" in high school.*

Fuck that.

I'm out.

There was no planning. I just went straight for worst-case scenario, slamming my head against the wall in front of my parents. Then everything went black. It happened so fast. It's almost like time shifted. And then I woke up in a small bed surrounded by babies getting out of brain surgery in the NICU at Children's Memorial Hospital in Chicago. It was horrible.

The second time I failed at killing myself, I was a business owner, a husband, and a father. Back then, I was drinking way too much and carrying around a lot of extra weight. I was barely surviving, but no one knew. On the outside looking in, I had it all.

I was recognized in my field as a celebrity hairdresser after placing as a finalist on the Bravo television show *Shear Genius*. I was getting paid to travel and speak while running multiple successful businesses. My clients were happy, my family loved me, the money was coming in …

And I was on my way out.

No amount of fame, fortune, or family could compete with the level of burnout I was experiencing from constantly putting out fires and taking care of everyone but myself.

If I hadn't sat down at the kitchen table that first day of April, 2018, looked at my wife, Angie, and said I was gonna do something stupid, my tombstone would have read:

BENJAMIN ROBERT MOLLIN
11/29/1974 — 04/01/2018

Instead, Angie kept me home to keep an eye on me. She loves me more than the world and didn't want to see me miserable. I told her I wanted to quit. Shut down the salon. Come home and have time with my family.

She saw what the salon was doing to me and told me to go ahead and quit. She could sense that if something didn't change, she was going to lose me as her husband and the father of our child.

Later, she shared with me a documentary on Netflix called *The Iron Cowboy*. It was cool, but what I didn't realize is that watching it changed my algorithm. All of a sudden, YouTube started showing me stuff about athletes.

When a video came on about athletes with disabilities, I sat there watching people who were missing limbs push their bodies to their limits. I started crying uncontrollably. I couldn't stop. Something in me shifted. All my self-pity started to crumble.

I figured if people without legs could compete in the Paralympic Games, I could push myself to do an IRONMAN® triathlon.

It nearly killed me, but I did it.

After the IRONMAN, I thought, *I'm going to get a tattoo of the IRONMAN logo, but I'm going to get it right on my f'n Adam's apple because if I can do an IRONMAN, I can take this pain, right? Nothing's gonna be worse than what I just went through.*

Wrong.

There's no color in that tat because I turned soft real quick when that needle went in.

Since then, I've gone on to run multiple ultramarathons. I went from a kid who used to play in a punk band with sold-out shows to getting myself into massive debt to starring in *Shear Genius.* Then I became a burned out, overweight, functioning alcoholic about to off himself. Now I'm an endurance athlete and a suicide prevention specialist.

If I can go from being a hairdresser to an ultrarunner and from suicidal to helping people not kill themselves, you can become anything. *Anything.* I just had to learn that instead of pointing the gun at myself, I could point it at the shit that was killing me and end my career instead of my life.

Sometimes you've got to destroy everything around you that's weighing you down and everything in you that's holding you back to unleash your inner warrior.

Trigger Warnings

The deeper you get into this book, the more graphic and irreverent it's going to get.

People are always in a good mood when they're sneezing or farting or eating, right? If not, they probably just need a good laugh. If you can make somebody laugh, they forget all about their world. Whatever they've got going on just seems to disappear.

When I don't know what to do, my default is to make it funny. The overall hatred that I have for all things f'n corporate (or pretty much anything that's not punk rock) I usually find a way to make it sarcastic and turn that sarcasm into humor.

Laughter is the ultimate factory reset.

I love offensive shit, but if you're easily offended by things like profanity, alcohol, drugs, or death, you might want to put this book down or give it to someone else. Probably best if it goes to someone with a warped sense of humor.

> On a serious note, for those of you reading this who know me, please know that I love you. But more importantly, I love and forgive myself for feeling the way that I did. I am a work in progress until I die of natural causes.
>
> —Ben

If you or someone you know struggles with depression or suicide ideation, there is hope. To reach a 24/7 crisis line:

Text the word HOME to 741-741.

For immediate assistance, please dial 911.

CELEBRITY

"In the future, everyone will be world-famous for fifteen minutes."

—Andy Warhol

The Road to *Shear Genius*

At no time in my life did I ever talk to a therapist about my first suicide attempt. My parents and I literally swept it under the rug and chalked it up as a loss. I noticed that they were just different around me. I was treated with a weird type of seniority.

As an artist and eccentric individual who is also a suicide survivor, I have some pretty interesting internal dialogue. I mean, I still do normal things. But back then, it was sort of like I got into a car accident or something, but not everybody knew about it. Only the people who were really close to me knew, so all of a sudden, it turned into this very, very private thing.

My mom would say things like, “Hey, you doing OK? Just checking in.”

And I’d be like, “I’m here. I’m cool.”

It wasn’t something we talked about that much. We just kind of brushed it off because we were close.

I never really thought about death, but at times, I would risk my life for thrill seeking and enjoyment. Anything less was just super boring.

My buddy Chris and I would get in the car and go 80 miles an hour on the expressway and switch seats by going over the roof.

We did this multiple times. One false move, and we would have been slaughtered.

There was also the time I almost got into a motorcycle accident on the expressway coming home from a PRIDE parade while wearing a boa.

From skydiving on mushrooms to driving motorcycles at 180 mph in shorts and flip-flops, I've got to admit, the fact that I'm not dead blows my mind.

Whenever I felt trapped in the house, I knew I had to do something, so I did something risky or creative every day.

In 1992, I got my first tattoo and played "Smells Like Teen Spirit" at my high school talent show. In the early 2000s, I was playing in original bands, cover bands, and with Chicago blues legend Bobby "Slim" James.

I landed commercial work in the city and even did hair for a couple of movies.

My film career was incredibly interesting. A woman named Lee Jones landed me a spot doing hair for a feature film called *5-25-77*, which is the day *Star Wars* came out. I lived in an Econolodge for a month doing hair for the cast.

It was directed by some dude named Patrick Reed Johnson. I believe he made an episode for that Fraggle Rock-type show *Dinosaurs*, back in the day. You know, the one with the little dinosaur that says, "Not the mama!"

This movie was about Patrick as a teenager. It starred an actor by the name of John Francis Daley. You might remember him from *Freaks and Geeks* and *Waiting*. We instantly hit it off, even stayed friends for a little while after filming.

The same woman who got me that gig also got me a hair gig working on *Drunkboat*, starring John Malkovich and Dana Delany. John Goodman was in it, too, but I never met him—probably because he doesn't like to be touched (at least, that's what I've heard).

Instead of being hired for the whole movie, I was hired for a reshoot of some specific scenes. The movie was being filmed in Chicago, so I would just drive in and drive home.

Although John Malkovich is bald, he came equipped with some crazyass high-end toupee of sorts, which apparently was woven by an Austrian man (maybe a Swiss man?) and hand sewn with yak hair. This was handed to me in a padded manilla envelope at a production meeting the day prior to filming.

I remember opening it up when I got home and thinking, *What the fuck is this? Ah, shit. I'm in over my head. What the hell am I supposed to do with this? I'm gonna look like an asshole in front of an A-list celebrity.*

The makeup artist knew what to do. She pinned it to a headform like the previous hairdresser had done. Then, in comes John Malkovich. He walks right up to the headform, applies adhesive to his head, takes off the yak toupee, puts it on himself, and hands me the mirror so he can see the back.

Then he hands me a toothbrush and says that as long as I've got the mirror and the toothbrush, we're cool. The mirror was to see how it looked, and the toothbrush was to gently comb this majestic beast. My job was to follow him around the movie set all day.

All my life, I've been a hustler and an artist.

When I was 21, I figured out how to take $16,000 and turn it into nearly a quarter of a million dollars gross annual revenue along with a $100k salary—for two or three years—without college, without anything.

So what does a 21-year-old do with that kind of money? He travels the world, lives out his wildest dreams for a couple years, then sells the business, buys a record store, and loses everything. It was a wild ride.

My best friend at the time was Alan. He was my roommate and travel buddy. He was dating a girl who lived in Amsterdam, so I flew out there to visit him. We hung out for a week, and by sheer luck, ended up bumping into Radiohead at a coffee shop.

Alan's girlfriend worked as a casting agent for the European MTV Music Awards, and I actually got invited to be part of the audience, like one of those people you see dancing at halftime during the Super Bowl. But I couldn't make it work with my business commitments, so I had to head back.

When I was making money, I was gone. I'd go as far as I could, staying in $400-a-night hotels in places like Holland. Eating at 3 a.m. and gaining weight from my awful diet, I ended up seeing a proctologist for internal hemorrhaging. I was basically living like Elvis.

At 23, I had $100,000 in cash saved up. Between my businesses and selling weed, I was doing well. I wouldn't sell to anyone under 50, just pre-rolled joints. It was this whole experience.

They'd come in, I'd touch up their hair, and we'd smoke a bowl while listening to Fleetwood Mac or *Dreamboat Annie*—some nostalgic music that took them back to high school. They'd tell stories, we'd laugh, and six weeks later, they'd come back for more.

I had a machine that rolled joints like a cigarette press, and my top drawer was always stocked. Some people in salons sold shampoo; I sold pre-rolls at a 600% markup.

Drugs were always around, and we lost a few in our circle to overdoses, but my mom told me early on never to do a drug I wouldn't tell her about. It worked.

I was more of a weed, alcohol, and mushrooms kind of guy. However, I was no angel. On weekends, I would sometimes experiment with other drugs, but that didn't last too long. Thank God I never got addicted.

Then came the record store. That was a disaster. I ended up $100,000 in debt, rocking the fuck out, running shit salons, and opening a record store right about the time everything started to go digital.

There was no light at the end of the tunnel. I figured I could either file for bankruptcy or become famous.

That's when I had the greatest idea. I wanted to make a documentary/mockumentary about hairdressers and sell it.

In 2007, I started looking for salons in Xenia, Ohio, and other Midwest regions to do a *Gummo* type thing. *Gummo* is my favorite movie of all time. It's dark in a way that is next level. The director's name is Harmony Corrine, and Xenia, Ohio, is the town where Gummo was filmed.

I wanted to film different beauty salons and call it *Hair to the Throne*. I needed to make some money and somehow become famous in the process. Becoming a celebrity was the biggest Hail Mary, but I figured, *what the fuck*, at this point in my life, I was fearless.

We started mapping out some locations and pulling together a production crew. At least, that was my plan. Plan B (otherwise known as Plan Bankruptcy) was going to be followed by an unstrategic move out West.

Before this journey, I gave myself a challenge. Because I had been self-employed for so long, I needed to know if I was actually any good. So, for my own ego, I googled "Top Chicago Salon." Whatever showed up, I was going to go there and apply.

A salon in the Gold Coast of Chicago was the first listing, so I called them up and said, "Hey, I live in Calumet City, I've worked on movies, and I work from home. I'm looking to step into more of a high-end salon because I'm only 25 minutes from Chicago."

Of course, I didn't tell them I didn't want the job, was $100,000 in debt, or that I was planning to make the hairdressing version of *Gummo*. My plan was to become a celebrity, but first, I wanted to see if I was any good at doing hair—at least good enough to work in a major city at a nice salon.

I had always told myself, "Worst case scenario, if music doesn't work, I can move anywhere in the world and cut hair." Now it was time to see if I could.

So I go into this place, and they have me bring in three models. I had to do a haircut, a color, and a men's cut.

Two days later, I get a phone call—I got hired as a top stylist. Hairdressing has all these adjectives to describe your experience and skill level, and I landed at the top tier. I was thinking, *Okay, cool. I'm good.*

Now, I had zero intention of taking this job. I just wanted to see if I could show up as this random stoner dude cutting hair out of his living room and get hired at some posh-ass salon in a major city.

The day I was supposed to start, I never showed up. One of the owners called, and I answered with, "Yeah, I was never really gonna come in. I just wanted to see if I could get hired. Man, I'm sorry. Kind of a prick move on my end." Then we hung up.

A couple days later, I get a message on MySpace from one of their colorists. She goes, "Hey, heard what you did. F'n legend. Let's hang out."

If you were a rich, white, suburban girl who wanted to be rebellious, I was exactly the guy you'd bring home. Want to piss off your parents? I'm your rebel flag. I mean, I was the kind of guy who would talk shit to their dad if he was giving me shit.

Back then, I was a wildcard—tons of tattoos, full-on punk-rock Jew (which is different from actually being Jewish because my Calabrese Italian mom was only Jewish by injection since my dad was a super Jew). Getting tattooed ruled. I loved everything about it. I got inked up once in a kitchen of an outlaw biker and went to Gary, Indiana, to get tattooed by Roy Boy. They had tigers in the basement.

Somehow, I even got paid to drink. Agencies would pay guys like me to go to bar openings and make the place look cooler. At one point, I almost ended up in a Marlboro catalog, posing at a nightclub with other dudes who looked like me, smoking cigarettes. I did make it into *Chicago Magazine* once, though.

A few days after hearing from the colorist on MySpace, my buddy John texts me and says, "You want to do a tryout for *America's Next Top Talent*?"

I'm thinking, *What the hell? The universe just opened up.*

I tell him, "Dude, I'm gonna be in Chicago anyway. I'm supposed to hang out with this girl I met at a salon."

He says, "Perfect. What time will you be out here?"

I'm all, "Just tell me where and when."

Then he says, "If you know anybody else who might be a good fit for it, let me know."

So I call a guy named Derek, a lounge singer with this cool Dean Martin vibe, and I say, "Hey, I've got these auditions for *America's Next Top Talent*. Let's see what happens."

My buddy John, who was working in the TV and film industry in Chicago, was part of the mix too. He's the guy who adopted my old pit bull, Bella.

So I show up, and I end up singing a Sam Cooke song in front of everyone, while Derek belts out "Misty," an old classic. That was it. They took our info, and we were done. Then I hop in a cab, lose my phone, and somehow still end up meeting the salon girl at a bar in the city.

Meanwhile, back in Calumet City, I keep working on *Hair to the Throne*, advertising heavily on Craigslist, looking for talent.

The girl I had met at the fancy-ass Chicago salon ends up having a client in her chair who was a producer from Los Angeles. They get to chatting, and she mentions what I'm working on. I think she may have even shown her my Craigslist ad.

That producer, Joan O'Connor, reaches out to me via email and says, "If you're serious about *Hair to the Throne*, you're going to need to establish yourself as a celebrity. And, by the way, there's an open audition coming up for hairdressers—can you put together a resume and some references?"

I was like, "Yeah, I can do that." I told her about Lee Jones, the woman who was hiring me for freelance gigs and regularly put me in rooms with celebrities to do their hair. Joan must've seen the potential, and soon after that, I'm emailing back and forth with Bravo's production team for a competition show called *Top Hair*.

One day, while I'm in Chicago driving around by myself, about to grab tapas and Sangria, Bravo calls me out of the blue. They say, "You got a minute?"

I say, "Yeah, I've got all day."

Then they hit me with: "If you had to leave for a couple of months, could you pack everything up and go?"

Without missing a beat, I say, "I'll start driving right now. Just give me the address."

Dead silence.

I'm like, "No, really. My life right now makes me look like a carny. I'm $100,000 in debt, living in a band house, and about to attempt to dress like a 1970s pimp from the South Side of Chicago. My plan is to find the most interesting hairdressers around the area where *Gummo* was filmed and make a documentary/mockumentary. I'm calling it *Hair to the Throne*. That's how I'm gonna get out of debt."

They were laughing so hard, and one of them says, "We have to meet you in person."

So I show up to the hotel where they're holding open auditions, and the producers have me tell them hair stories—just wild, ridiculous hair stories.

I talk about the clients who had shit their pants while I was doing their hair and the time I had to measure a rather obese naked woman. I'm all … "Have you ever seen Pat from SNL? Put some extra weight on that with some double Fs for 'Flapjack Flapjack' and a Ryan Seacrest haircut. Now measure it. Naked."

I didn't hold back, and they were cracking up the entire time. They loved it. Then they hit me with, "Protocol is protocol. Can you make an audition video and send us a DVD?"

I had recently made a song called "Haircuts in the Summer" with my buddy DK. It was just something fun to do, but now I thought, *This could be my ticket.*

I immediately called my friend Nick, who I'd met a couple of years earlier, working on the film *5-25-77*. He lived in Detroit, four hours away.

When he answered, I said, "Nick, I need a huge favor. I think I'm a lock for a Bravo reality show, but I need your help to make a killer video. Can you pack up your gear and drive to my house? We'll stay up for two days straight if we have to."

He didn't even hesitate—he was on his way. Honestly, if it wasn't for Nick, I don't think I'd be where I am today.

Nick followed me around all day while we filmed the video for *Haircuts in the Summer*. We stayed up for a day and a half straight to finish it.

It ended up being a hip-hop video of me cutting hair, doing Bikram yoga, smoking weed, hanging with my clients—this dude named Earl and an older lady who was getting a touch-up.

Once it was done, Nick and I drove to the Calumet City post office, and I sent it off to Bravo.

Afterward, I thought, "Man, did I screw that up? I should've just kept it simple. They're probably watching the video like, 'Who the hell is this guy and WTF is he doing?'"

And then, radio silence.

I eventually got an email saying they received the video, but nothing else. A month went by, so I called them.

They said, "Hey, man, just stay positive. We're rooting for you so hard. We *need* you on this show. That video was f'ing epic—we walk around singing that song!"

Then, in the winter of 2006, I get a frantic phone call: "Can you send us pictures of your most current work?"

Using one of those old purple Best Buy digital cameras—this was before phones had decent cameras—I snapped a picture of the client I was working on right then.

She looked kind of like Mary J. Blige, and we did her hair cool AF. I sent that over, and four days later, I got a FedEx package full of disclosure and confidentiality agreements. I signed everything, mailed it back, and two days after that, I had a plane ticket in hand.

I packed all my bags, borrowed a guitar from this dude Dave, and my dad dropped me off at the airport.

Hollywood? Holy Shit.

The plane ride was surreal. I was on my way to Hollywood.

Once I landed, a production assistant picked me up in a big white utility truck. He drove me to an airport hotel, got me checked in, and brought me to my room. I was told to relax—but not to leave. I had to stay put until I got further instructions.

Then they handed me a psychological evaluation form to fill out. I was also told that when they came back, my phone would eventually be confiscated.

A few hours later, someone came to get me. They grabbed the form and led me down the hall into a room with two mannequin heads. There was another contestant on the other side of a divider in the room. We couldn't see each other.

I was given ten minutes to complete an updo on one of the mannequins. All I could think was, *Fuck. I hate doing updos.* I was nervous, but I stayed cool. I did a French twist kind of thing and hoped it was enough.

Next up, they interviewed me on camera. Looking back now, I can see they were already testing us in the format of the show.

Every time I got interviewed, it went really well. I didn't try to be anything I wasn't. I was just myself. Besides, they already felt how awesome I was from my "Haircuts in the Summer" audition. I would hear the crew randomly sing a line while they were filming, and it cracked me up every time.

Later on, they brought me into a room with all the producers. I had them laughing hysterically again.

Then they gave me my phone and sent me back to my room.

The next morning, I got the news: I made the show.

No f'n way. I'm gonna be on a reality competition doing hair.

First place is $100,000.

Game on.

That same morning, they took my phone away for good—at least for the rest of filming.

The 12 of us (the 11 other contestants and me) were taken into a small conference room. It was the first time we saw each other. Nobody said anything.

A lawyer stood in front of the room and walked us through our confidentiality agreements. We were not allowed to talk—about the show or the results. If we did, there'd be serious financial consequences.

We signed a bunch of papers, then piled into a passenger van and got driven to a studio. We weren't allowed to talk or interact with each other until the cameras started rolling.

First stop: filming the commercials for *Shear Genius*. At some point along the way, they dropped the name *Top Hair*.

Filming the promos was awesome. Kind of surreal. This was also the first time we met Jaclyn Smith. She was on set the entire time.

We did more interviews and said "Only on Bravo" over and over again for the commercials.

Then they brought us to the place we'd be living for the rest of the shoot. It was a big warehouse loft with communal bunk beds, a pool table, a kitchen, and one big open common area. The fridge was stocked with food, beer, wine, and a bottle of Patrón Silver.

It felt a little like *The Real World*, but not as fancy. I grabbed a top bunk. I don't think any of us slept that night.

The next morning, breakfast showed up, and we all got back in the van and went to the filming location.

The second we stepped out of the van, cameras were on us.

We walked into the *Shear Genius* set, and just like that, the competition began.

I couldn't believe it was actually happening.

The whole time I was thinking, *OMG. I'm gonna be on TV. Wow. Just wow.*

Confined and Competing

Season 1 of *Shear Genius* had eight episodes and a reunion show. If you want to check out the breakdown, it's all still online. Since I was runner-up, I made it through all eight episodes, plus the reunion. That means I was on TV every single week for nine straight weeks, but the show aired for seven years in 44 different countries.

We shot the whole season in just over a month with only three off-days the entire time. On one of them, I went longboarding in Venice Beach with Tyson. Another day, I hit a Bikram yoga class with Daisy.

The last break came when we were down to the final four—me, Dr. Boogie, Daisy, and Anthony. We watched the Bears vs. Colts game at The Abbey in LA, and Prince played the halftime show. I'll never forget it.

Outside of those three days, we were filming non-stop. Long-ass days. Constant pressure. No real breaks. It was intense as hell.

It's been so long, most of the details are fuzzy now, but I do remember some of the drama and the rhythm of how it worked.

Each episode followed a formula: there'd be a "short cut challenge"—basically a shorter, less-involved assignment. If you won that, you'd get some kind of edge in the elimination challenge.

Then we'd film for like 16 to 18 hours straight, get maybe 8 to 10 hours off, and then right back at it.

After filming, we'd sit around in isolation trailers, waiting to find out who was going home. They did it to build suspense. You start to lose your shit a little bit in a setup like that.

Part of our contract was total isolation from the outside world—no communication. That was new for me. At the time, my mom was becoming more and more physically disabled, and my grandma wasn't doing well. I carried that with me the whole time.

Shear Genius became our world. We ate together. Slept in shared quarters. Rode in the same van to the shoot. And every time we rolled out for an elimination challenge, one person wouldn't be riding back.

Paul-Jean was the first to go during Episode 1. The challenge was to create a statement piece using random tools and props. Honestly, I thought he could've won the whole damn thing. Dude worked at a high-end salon in Beverly Hills. He had style, an eye for detail, and clean finishing work. He even let me borrow one of his designer suits during filming. I returned it when it was all over.

That week's guest judge was Frédéric Fekkai. I'd heard of him before—big name in Beverly Hills. Seemed arrogant to me. I think he was French?

I landed in the middle of the pack that episode and went back to the loft. With no outside contact, your whole reality becomes that set, those people, and whatever drama you're filming.

Every day was the same. Wake up, shower, breakfast shows up, then off to work. We'd load into the van and head out for whatever the day had in store.

For the most part, the living quarters were chill. But after the episode where Evangeline used hedge trimmers to cut hair, there was some off-camera heat. I remember her and Tabatha going at it. Tempers were quick to flare—with the pressure, the filming schedule, and the total isolation, it was mental fuckery at its finest.

Each day, we left, and each day, we came back, minus one.

I clicked with Anthony, Tabatha, and Daisy right away. The rest of the cast were all cool in their own way, but I just vibed with those three. Tabatha especially—I really liked her.

I usually did well in the short cut challenges. It was the elimination challenges where I found myself on thin ice.

The first time I really thought I was out was Episode 4, the Red Carpet Challenge. We had to get our models glammed up like they were headed to a red carpet event. I got one of the last model picks, a beautiful African-American woman, but as soon as I chose her, she told me all her hair was sewn-in extensions.

I acted like I had it under control, but the second I applied heat, nothing held. I knew I was fucked.

I looked around—everyone else had these polished, stunning looks. Mine looked like she just had breakup sex and then went horseback riding.

Evangeline's wasn't much better. Her model looked wild.

That week's guest judge was Vanessa Williams. Remember the song, "Save the Best for Last"? That was my senior prom song.

Anyway, they called out the bottom two—me and Evangeline. I remember just laughing. I was ready to go home. But somehow, I made it through, and Evangeline and her garden shears were out.

Each episode I survived, I was one step closer. The waiting after every challenge was brutal. Isolation while you're awaiting your fate is no joke, and I needed that $100k bad.

When I felt like I was bombing a challenge, I'd look around and see who was struggling and focus on staying in the game. I didn't need to be the best. Just not the worst. I still kind of live that way—I'm not going for the best, just better than most.

Eventually, it came down to the final three: Daisy, Anthony, and me. For the last challenge, we had to create three different looks on three models and tell a story.

The guest judge was Vidal F'ing Sassoon. I did an off-the-face updo, a bob, and a disconnected, razored, layered haircut. My story was about the shift from inner beauty to outer beauty.

After we presented, we got sent back to our trailers to wait. And then came the knock. It was Vidal Sassoon at my trailer door.

"Would you mind if I came in?" he asked.

I was eating carryout chicken chop suey and offered him a plate. He took it. What followed was one of the biggest moments of my career. We talked for over an hour.

I asked him how he got started. He asked me where I was from. We talked about my parents, my upbringing. He told me I had raw talent and needed to refine it and that I should become an educator. I asked if he was just saying that because he was Vidal Sassoon. He laughed. "No, I mean it," he said.

That was it. That's when I felt like I'd already won.

Daisy got eliminated first. Then it was just Anthony and me. We held hands, waited for the call. For over a month, it had been nonstop filming, long days, no contact with the outside world. We were tired and hungry.

When they finally called Anthony as the winner, I felt relief. I was genuinely happy for him. Still love that dude.

That night, we sipped champagne and finally let our hair down. The next day, I flew back to Chicago. I was the runner-up on the first season of *Shear Genius*.

Nobody knew where I'd been or what I was doing for over a month. I kept thinking, "People are gonna freak." And they did.

WTF

Three months before I left to film for a month, I witnessed a drive-by shooting while smoking a cigarette on my front porch. It was right across the street.

Seeing it happen, rather than just hearing about it, made everything feel so real and terrifying. Even though my block had always felt pretty chill, that's when I knew it was time to move.

With the steady decline of my mom and grandma, I needed to stay close enough to help them if needed. I was on my own with that.

In 2007, it was easy to buy a house with no money. I found a super old, small house in a great neighborhood for a great price. Someone had flipped it, and it was way nicer than any area I'd ever lived in.

So I took out a high-interest loan, rented my old house to Nick (the guy who made my audition DVD), and with a few signatures, I became a resident in Munster, IN. I had hardly anything in my old house, so moving in was a breeze.

The first thing I did was have a shampoo bowl installed in one of the rooms. I've had a home studio the whole time I've been doing hair, even when I owned salons. Give a haircut, sell some weed. Man, I miss those days.

I moved and set up camp in about two weeks once I got back. I still did the same clients I had in my Cal City house, but now I was set up at my new house.

Then I got a phone call from Tabatha.

She said, "So, what are you going to do now?"

"Hmmm, I don't know, just go back to seeing clients, I guess."

She told me that I should start working for a product company. She and Anthony had been working for one named Joico for a while, so she made the introduction.

Meanwhile, a brand called Nexxus, which was owned by Alberto Culver, was looking to hire me to do celebrity-type work for them.

One day, I get a text from a family friend, a doctor named Alan Ruby, who was on a business trip. He was walking around New York and noticed an ad for *Shear Genius* on the side of a bus. It was of me, but it was photoshopped to look like I was climbing some hair. He took a picture of it and sent it to me.

Then, on his flight back to Chicago, he texted me from the plane and sent me a screenshot of what he was watching. It was a commercial for *Shear Genius*.

I was in shock. This was about a month or so after I got back from filming.

Bravo had started airing commercials, and I was in them. That's when it hit me. *I'm about to be on TV. Me.*

Almost overnight, the phone calls started.

"Hey man, you gonna be on Bravo?"

"Yeah, but I'm not supposed to talk about it."

More commercials, more ads, and then all of a sudden, *People* magazine and *TV Guide*. Even before the show aired, I was blowing up.

It wasn't uncommon for me to get back-to-back phone calls and messages from everyone I'd ever met. Same question: "Hey man, are you gonna be on *Shear Genius*?"

I had no clue what to expect.

Little did I know that life as I knew it was never going to be the same.

Bravo Famous

I got to see the first episode of the show on April 11, 2007, at a brewery near my house called 3 Floyds Brewing, one of the top places in the world to drink beer. They threw a viewing party for me. It was surreal.

I drove up and there were tons of people, a news camera, and all kinds of cool shit. I'm actually getting choked up just thinking about it.

I took a seat, and then the show aired. In the intro of the show, when I came up and my name flashed on the screen, the place went ape shit. My mom cried the whole time.

I couldn't believe it. I was on TV. And I was the only one that knew I was gonna be on all the episodes.

The next day, I became a celebrity. That's the only way to explain it. It was an overnight thing.

Social media back then was MySpace, which I always had for music, but hair was different. All of a sudden, I got 10,000 new followers and tons of messages. It was nuts. My phone would ring all day, and it wasn't uncommon to receive text messages throughout the night.

Nexxus and Joico contacted me around the same time to represent them. Nexxus asked if I had an agent or a manager, which I did not.

I contacted a guy named Mike, who was managing a buddy of mine's band called "The Steepwater Band." Mike was awesome. He had a cowboy thing about him and was both smart and a badass. I felt good with him.

We met with Nexxus in Chicago, and I brought Mike. They wanted me to go on celebrity TV and show people at home how to style their hair using Nexxus products. An "Even you can have celebrity hair at home" kind of thing.

They were gonna pay me thousands of dollars a day.

I spoke with Mike about it and didn't feel comfortable being "that" guy. So I declined. It didn't make sense for me to be so far out of my comfort zone. I would have felt like a tool.

Soon after that, I was on a plane ride to LA to meet with Joico. The meeting went well. They took me out for sushi, then out for drinks, and that's when I met my soon-to-be mentor, Addam. He was basically the love child of David Bowie and Blondie.

Joico seemed like a good fit, so after a handshake, I was on board.

The show continued to air. Every week, there was a new episode. Every time I'd walk into a new viewing party at a local restaurant or bar, I'd get cheers. People loved the show.

Now this whole time, I was cutting hair in a makeshift salon in the back of my buddy's guitar shop, and I had a Comcast digital phone that never stopped ringing. People from all over the country were looking for appointments.

I hired someone to answer the phone, and I didn't do the same client twice. Every day, it was a *Shear Genius* fan wanting a haircut and to talk about the show.

I'd never been that busy behind the chair.

My grandma was still alive, and she was my biggest fan. There's even a pre-recorded video of her during one of the final episodes of the show. The moment I saw her and my mom and heard their voices, I lost it. Yep, I broke down and cried on national television.

I was still playing in bands. This is when the no-days-off started.

In the hair world, we have hair/trade shows which are thrown in convention centers all over the US and globally.

My first actual hair show was in Chicago at the Americas Beauty Show. I was with Tabatha and Anthony, and we were all working for Joico.

We were getting mobbed. At certain points, we even needed security. It was insane. We were like The Beatles.

I'll never forget what that felt like.

I was being groomed to become a platform artist and educator. I was down. It was so out of my everyday life, but it felt natural in an unnatural way.

I know that's confusing, but it's the only way I can explain it.

Every day, I'd get stopped, be photographed, and then it would happen again. If I went to Target, it would happen every time, same at the bank.

Eventually, news outlets would call, and I'd do a lot of interviews. I couldn't believe that this was my life.

After filming, Bravo gave us access to a psychiatrist for a full year. I think his name was Brian. I checked in with him a few times. I'd tell him I felt bad for actual famous people. If this is what being Bravo famous gets you, I can't even imagine being Brad Pitt.

My mom saved everything. All the media, magazines, and news clippings. I have a box in my basement where all of that lives.

Right around Episode 5, the whole cast flew back to LA to film a reunion show with Andy Cohen. After the reunion show, we all went out to party.

We were treated like celebrities in LA, and I partied like a rock star—with actual rock stars—that night.

I still can't believe that I was given that opportunity, and I can't believe I almost won.

I find it crazy that some people still look at me as a famous person. Honestly? It cracks me up.

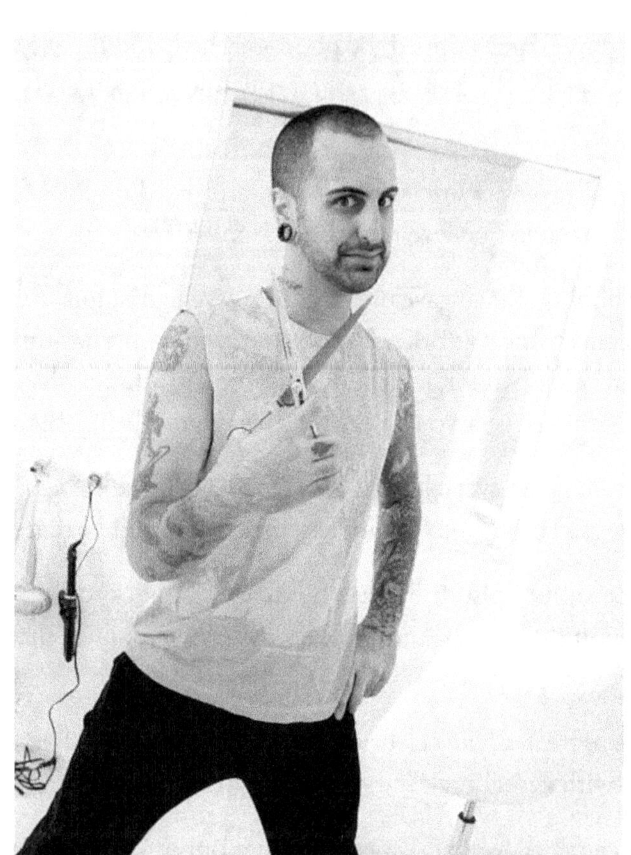

Ben Mollin, tatted and gauged,
wielding cutting shears on the set of Shear Genius
(Photo courtesy of Bravo, Shear Genius, 2007)

Would I ever do it again?

Abso-f'n-lutely.

CREATIVITY

**"They laugh at me because I'm different.
I laugh at them because they're all the same."**

—largely attributed to Kurt Cobain

Shit Got Real Before Shit Got Real

I moved to Indiana from the drive-by house, got courthouse married, and opened up a salon. Around that time, the TV stuff started happening, and life became a whirlwind. It didn't take long for me to realize my marriage was toxic.

After about a year and a half, I left. Thirty minutes after getting my separation papers, I met Angela Avorio (more about that in the "Family" section). We hit it off immediately and got married a year later. That was 14 years ago.

During that time, I was busier than ever as a hairstylist—everyone wanted me to do their hair. Clients would sometimes open up about heavy topics, like suicide or funerals they'd be attending.

Anytime I'd open up and share my own story of attempting suicide when I was a kid, something shifted in the conversations. Or when I would tell them that at 21, my best friend Alan killed himself, people just looked at me differently.

They listened more, respected what I had to say, and often wanted to hug me. I wanted those hugs, too.

Despite all my success, I found myself stuck in a grind I didn't know how to escape—no days off from 2007 to 2018. Eleven years after becoming a celebrity hairstylist, I was trapped in a life I hated. I felt so lost, I even started planning my own death.

Before we go there, let's go back to the beginning of my creative journey ...

The Birth of an Artist

I never really knew who I was, but I knew I was different.

Back when I was about 15 (I don't think I was driving yet), I had this humanities teacher named Mr. Kruzan. He was my first openly gay teacher, and he had a boyfriend named Lee.

He would take our humanities class out to different restaurants around Chicago, and if we tried something he ordered off the menu, we'd earn extra credit points. We'd go to Japanese restaurants, traditional Mexican places, German, Italian—you name it. He was giving us Southside kids a taste of culture, and it had a huge impact on me.

I loved learning about humanities, artwork, and concepts like chiaroscuro, where you use dark areas around a light subject to make it stand out. I even used this technique a lot as a hairdresser to teach color placement. If you want something to pop, put it next to something dark.

One day, we had a poetry assignment. We had to go to the library, find a poem we liked, then take a poster board, write the poem out, and draw a picture representing how we felt about it. I found a short poem about plums and an icebox.

I didn't put much thought into it. I grabbed a poster board, drew a basket, wrote "author unknown," and sprayed some shellac on it to make it look a little more presentable, in case they wanted to frame it.

So I go back to school, and he's handing back our assignments. I didn't get mine back. He says, "Can you stay after class?" I thought he was going to call me out for just throwing it together at the last minute.

But after class, I walk up to him, and he's looking sincere. He hands me a 50-dollar bill and says, "I want to buy that off you. That was my favorite poem when I was in college. Now, if anyone ever asks what you do, you can tell them you're an artist."

From that point on, I started telling people I was an artist because I had permission from an adult. It was one of the most pivotal moments of my life.

Blinded by Cigarette Hands

When I started beauty school at about 17, I didn't know much. Aside from giving a classmate a spiral perm in the tenth grade, I had never really done hair. I mean, I'd give myself swim-team haircuts, and I knew how to do a French braid and shit like that, but I couldn't figure out color.

And then, all of a sudden, it clicked. In my head, the memory of taking saxophone lessons as a 12-year-old kid came flooding back. That's the year my parents decided I should probably start playing jazz.

My mom knew about this saxophone player who was teaching lessons from his house. What my mom didn't know was that this guy was an f'n brilliant madman.

She'd drop me off at his house, and we'd head down to the basement. All he would do was smoke Marlboro Lights. If I try to trigger the smell memory, I believe he was drinking gin and tonics. And then he'd escape into the bathroom every couple of minutes. In my imagination, I'd picture him doing lines of blow the size of a small child, then coming back out.

He'd sit there and try to get me to play these scales, and I fucking hated playing scales. I just wanted to learn how to solo. I wanted to be Clarence Clemons who played saxophone for Bruce Springsteen and was one of my biggest musical influences at the time.

There was this commercial where Clarence Clemons was playing "America the Beautiful," and while he was playing, fire came out of the bell. I was just like, *Yes. That's me!*

I'd practice with my dad while he played piano. My dad and I played live on a couple of local access cable shows back in the day. He taught me all these Duke Ellington songs and how to read music out of this thing called the *Real Book*, which was basically jazz standards and classics.

Looking back now, I probably should've learned more scales because I'd be a much more dimensional player.

Anyway, one day, my parents drop me off, and they're gone for an hour. I'm in the basement with this guy, butchering my scales. I look at the sheet, but it just isn't clicking.

While smoking, he says, "Play it again, play it again, play it again." And finally, he's just like, "Fuck it." Something went off in him. He goes over to a stereo, puts on a record (I think it was Gato Barbieri), and cranks it.

"From now on, if you're not going to practice your scales, we're going to refer to everything as color and texture. Close your eyes."

Then he takes his Marlboro-stained hands and puts them over my eyes and says, "Pay attention. Listen to that. It's red and it's rough. Say it."

He was freaking me out, but I say, "It's red, and it's rough."

Then he goes back over to the record player. "This is smooth. This is blue, and it's flat. It's clear. It's glass. Listen to it."

I sit there and listen, and when the lesson finally ends, my mom comes to get me. She says, "Well, how was it?"

I say, "Never take me back to that house ever again. Fuck that guy. He scares the shit out of me."

Looking back, I should've been practicing. He was just taking away my sight and trying to make me think about things differently. But it ended up being one of the greatest life lessons I ever learned about creating.

I'm now able to do things in layers, create stuff based on adjectives and emotion. When I create something, I naturally want to convey it in color and texture rather than just through verbal content and demonstration. It's become the way that I'm wired.

That first time I struggled to figure out hair color, I envisioned myself in this guy's basement with his hands over my eyes and him saying, "If you can't see it, then create it. What color is it? It's red. It's dark red. What texture is it? It's wild, it's frizzy.

Now it's dark. It's black. It's smooth. Now it's the ocean; there's a wave in it. It's blue—like glass."

It finally clicked.

Beauty School in Black & White

When I started beauty school, I enrolled at John Amico's in Oak Forest, Illinois. It was an all-Black school with an all-white dress code. After a few weeks of basics, I started realizing I was the only white person enrolled. I felt like a tooth.

When I finally got to the cutting floor, I was given all the white clients, which were rare. One teacher pulled me aside and asked, "Have you ever thought about where you're gonna work after you graduate?" I figured I'd just find a place to do relaxers and blowouts.

The staff and students were cool as hell, but there was this one girl who was smoking hot. She was a preacher's daughter and lived with her family in the same apartment complex where I was a lifeguard.

I worked up the courage to ask her out, but her boyfriend (a 6'4" football player) drove up from Tennessee to beat my ass in the parking lot. He took one look at me but never threw a punch. I think he felt sorry for me. Either that, or he was blinded by my all-white uniform. Shortly afterward, I switched schools.

I ended up at Cameo Beauty Academy in Oak Lawn. Still had to wear all white. Still felt like prison. We all wore the same thing and ate together everyday. The only place to get food within walking distance was Subway, so that was my prison food. Every.damn.day.

We'd cut hair on old ladies, cheap clients, and weirdos. People smoked under the dryers, and we had them sign waivers. Sue and Herman Harrison ran the place, and Ms. Pat was the best teacher there—an old-school legend.

Beauty school was easily one of the best decisions I ever made, but it was also weird AF.

One memorable client was an elderly woman bussed in for a perm. Her hair was a mix of gray and old dye, and after processing, it smelled like burning fish sticks. The perm rods slid off, and her hair looked like a '70s Jheri curl.

Another client tried to pleasure herself during a shampoo.

Once, I had to give a facial to an extremely elderly woman whose face was inches away from my groin. It was kind of like giving a shoulder massage to a Cornish hen. It can be done, it's just … difficult.

I hated every minute of anything beyond cutting.

To make money, I was tattooing punk rockers and selling weed. When my mom found a bunch of weed in my undershirt drawer that I had planned to sell, that's when I officially moved out of the house I was raised in.

I'd randomly crash at the homes of my music buddies, either in their parents' basement or on the couch. I'd also stay at my parents' house once in a while. Someone would have a party, and I'd just crash on their floor, then go to beauty school.

To pay my car payment, I worked at a paintball skateboard shop called Bad Boy Toyz and hustled small amounts of marijuana. My buddy Chris and I did landscaping during the summer that year for cash.

At 18, I graduated from beauty school with 1,500 hours behind me. My first job came from a "rip the number off the paper" ad on the help-wanted corkboard in the beauty school breakroom. A salon called Carousel was looking for a hairdresser, and they were just down the block from the school. I went in for an interview and was hired on the spot. It was inside a plaza and was just an older woman and a couple of chairs.

A few days later, I went in for my first day. She had me do an all-over color on one of her clients. I remember for lunch, I had to eat from Subway—again. I was so sick of Subway, I never went back to that salon.

I later worked at Borics for maybe two weeks. After a friend told me Kurt Cobain died, I quit on the spot.

Down the street there was a Supercuts, where I got the best haircutting class of my life. Supercuts was busy, and I loved it. That's where I learned how to cut efficiently. On any given day, our clientele would range from a bus full of intellectually disabled teens to traveling carnival workers. There were people coming in from all walks of life.

Around this time, I joined the Armando Vasquez salon in Lansing, Illinois—a high-end place with a dress code. Armando, a soft-spoken artist, taught me Sassoon-inspired cuts, and it wasn't long before I became self-sufficient. Armando showed me how to make cuts look expensive, and I became the hairdresser I am today because of him.

As I was starting to get the hang of doing hair, I was also heavily involved in the music scene, playing in a ska band that was having success. Then, without warning, my childhood friend Antwan died.

He was in college and had a seizure in the tub. When his mom called me, she was wrecked. I went to the memorial, which was an all-Black gospel service in the city. It was like something you'd see in a movie—loud, raw, holy. I felt every ounce of it.

HAUNTED

“I see dead people.”

—Cole Sear
The Sixth Sense, (Shyamalan, 1999)

The Ghost Room

I was living like a rock star. I had an apartment right down the street from Armando Vasquez, and I was finally making decent money. I learned a fuck-ton about doing good hair. I also learned a lot about gay dudes.

It wasn't all sunshine and roses. Two people shit their pants on me within a month. Some kids came in posing as selling chocolate and smeared shit all over the walls. One night, I accidentally showed up to work still high from partying at Crowbar. That was horrible.

After my lease was up, I moved to Homewood, Illinois, into the coolest apartment in the world. My girlfriend at the time was from Lansing, another Chicago suburb, but was studying in London. I maxed out a credit card and went out there for a few weeks with the intent of not coming back. That was my first time going to Amsterdam, but it wouldn't be my last. It was epic.

The Homewood apartment was cool, except it had roaches and ghosts. I found the apartment through a hairdresser friend named Lyse and her boyfriend Aaron. They said, "Hey, we've got a room that's available for rent in our apartment, but it's the ghost room."

I'm like, "Ghost room? How much is it?"

They said, "$350 a month."

I'm thinking, *For $350 a month, hell, I don't care if an f'n dead woman is in there.* Then I find out it's right by the train station to get me downtown. Perfect.

The apartment was big and crazy old. It kind of had that old Chicago feel to it with wood floors and high ceilings and a really cool staircase.

So I moved my stuff in.

I had a bed, a *Mission Impossible* poster that somebody gave me, and a Kurt Cobain poster that said, "I hate myself and I want to die." The walls were plaster, so I couldn't really stick anything up without heavy amounts of duct tape.

I had one of those three-shelf wicker things that you would buy from Pier 1 back in the day. I had that in the corner, a dresser, and a black-and-white TV. That was my room. Possession-wise, that's literally all I had.

Very soon after I moved in, I noticed this room was just different.

I remember thinking, *What makes it cold in here?* So I asked Aaron. He said, "Well, you go in there sometimes, and it's colder, and then you'll hear a bell."

I thought nothing of it. Lyse burned sage for me before I moved in. But I'm like, whatever, you know, it's haunted. Okay, great.

They had two cats, and I had one that I rescued from my landlord at my last apartment in Lansing. The unit adjacent to mine had started to develop a nasty smell. Six days later, the body of an elderly man was found in bed alongside his trusty cat.

My landlord, this old Italian guy named Sam, comes walking out of the apartment holding an old Persian cat and says, "You want a cat?"

I'm like, "What are you gonna do with it?"

And he says, "I'm gonna hit it over the head with a shovel and throw it in the garbage."

I'm thinking, *No, no, no!* Terrified, I felt it necessary to rescue this cat. So I did. This thing smelled like hell's asshole, so I gave it a shampoo in the tub and named it Perry.

Later, I find out that it had grown hungry and eaten its deceased owner's lips, and now I'm thinking, *This cat's a man-eater.*

Perry and the other two cats never went into my room in the apartment. It's important to mention here that we all had locks on our bedroom doors.

I came home from work one day—I was still working at Armando's, the day spa in Lansing—and the Kurt Cobain poster (the one I had put up with a duct tape frame) had slid off the wall and was on the ground.

I'm thinking, *Huh?*

I've taped things to walls before, and I know things like material, temperature, and moisture can affect how well they stick. At first, I figured moisture was the issue, but then I noticed the *Mission Impossible* poster was still up.

That got me thinking: maybe it's just that wall. Maybe there's a hot water line behind it, causing humidity and messing with the adhesive. So, I put it back up and didn't think much of it.

A couple weeks later, I came home from work on a Saturday at 3:30 in the afternoon. I opened the door, and everything was exactly as I left it—except the heating vent cover was in the center of my bed.

The wall at the foot of my bed was about five feet away and ten feet high. There was a vent where the heat came through. But now, the vent cover had somehow unscrewed itself and landed perfectly in the middle of my bed.

I stood there, thinking, *We lock our doors. No one's breaking into my room.* Yet, there it was, completely symmetrical, like it had been placed there. I had no explanation.

It wasn't ripped or forced out, so I put it back up. Things just had this tendency to slide. But this thing, which was probably a solid two pounds, obviously had a tendency to fly. I said, "Okay, this is weird," thought a little bit about it, and went to bed.

I used to fall asleep with the old black-and-white TV on. At night, it was usually *I Love Lucy* or something similar. I wouldn't turn the sound on; it was just for a little light because the room was super dark. I was one of those kids who needed a nightlight and a sleep machine. So as an adult, I'd still have the TV on and just go to bed.

Perry the cat decided that night to sleep with me. I don't even know what time it was.

And before I tell you this story—disclaimer, okay?—I was not on drugs.

It was 1996, and I probably had a beer or two at this place called the Fifth Quarter, which was right downstairs. It was just a typical night. I had to be up in the morning and go back to work. I would've just hung out with my roommates, a couple of friends, and gone to bed.

On this night, I wake up to my cat making this crazy-ass noise.

I turn over and I see what almost looks like a charcoal drawing in the shape of an old dude with long hair, and a noose around his neck, with his arms out in front of him. It kind of looked like my band buddy Brett, who also had long hair. I thought I was dreaming. I remember yelling out, "Brett?"

When I realized what was happening, every muscle in my body locked up. Even telling this story now, I can still remember that feeling—like when you yawn too hard or pull your tongue and neck, and you feel it in your brain. My entire body was paralyzed. I literally couldn't move.

I was lying there, staring at the silhouette of this older man with long hair, hanging with his arms out, looking like the static on an old TV. My cat was going nuts. I don't remember much except that I couldn't move. The fear was completely paralyzing.

Somehow, I worked up the strength to push myself up, jerk upright, and flip over. As soon as I did, I felt a double slap on my legs. Then, it was like someone took the palms of their hands and swiped down from behind my knees to my feet as fast as they could. I was touched by this apparition.

I remember thinking, *I'm going to die.* I couldn't believe what was happening, and the whole time, my cat was still freaking out. I tried to scream, but nothing came out—I was too petrified. It was the craziest feeling.

Eventually, I did the same jerking motion again, rolled over, and looked at it. The figure disappeared, turning into an orange orb of light that rose into the air, went under the door, and vanished.

So I get up, butt-naked, and run into Lyse and Aaron's room, screaming, "Ghost! I saw a ghost!" Aaron wakes up and starts shouting. I'm jumping up and down with my dick in his face. It was a weird moment.

Then I went back into my room, and Aaron came with me. He kind of big-brothered me because I completely lost it.

I ended up going home to my parents' house and starting from scratch. The whole experience just freaked me out. I left everything in that apartment and never went back.

Nightmares

For a year, I had the worst dreams, and I would wake up screaming. Every.single.night.

In the nightmares, I'd be back in that room, being led to some other level of consciousness—as if the apparition wanted to show me what happened to him.

I'd have the same dream all the time where I was driving my mom's gray Oldsmobile Aurora. We'd be going up this mountain road and then drive off the edge. I'd wake up with that feeling of falling. Each time, I'd reach a different level, kind of like a video game.

Every night I'd go to bed, I'd have night terrors. It was always about someone I loved. I didn't know what to do. There was no internet to turn to back then, so I told my mom, "I can't live like this—I keep going back to the same dream every time I close my eyes, again and again."

I did some research, talked to people, even reached out to a paranormal group. From what I learned, when energy transfer is that powerful, it can disrupt your brain waves—especially when it involves touch. People who are intuitive have similar stories.

After about a year, I started having nightmares about this girl from grade school who had cancer. In my dream, her mouth would open and a demon would come out. It was messed up. Over time, it just faded away.

I believe someone took their life in that Homewood ghost room, alone, with no one to help their soul pass. A lot of frustration was bottled up in there. I'm no paranormal expert, but I'm sensitive to supernatural energy, and that was *intense*.

To this day, I have a sixth sense about evil and ghosts. Old houses, bars, hotels—I can immediately feel if something's haunted. And if I get that weird feeling, I won't go in.

The Dead Bird

The strain on my body from seeing the ghost in my room was crazy. My neck was screwed up for months, my feet ached, and my toes curled so tight the balls of my feet throbbed. It felt like I'd torn tendons in my throat. My neck, shoulders, armpits, toes—everything felt like whiplash—as if I'd been in a car accident. I couldn't turn my head for months.

Then, one day, I'm cutting hair in my salon, and out of nowhere, this bird just strolls in through the back door. It was a big black bird, not quite a crow, but close enough. I'm working away when it walks right up to me, gives me this look, and then—bam—drops dead at my feet.

I'm standing there like, "Are you kidding me? What does this mean?" I start freaking out a little, thinking maybe I've got to sacrifice something now or find some weird albino virgin. Like, what do I do? Should I bleed a chicken and pray to Santa Rita? I tossed a towel over it, threw it in the dumpster, and got back to cutting hair.

After the bird incident, things calmed down a bit. Maybe it was the pinnacle of that season. I don't know.

Colored by Death

My best friend in my mid-twenties was a guy named Alan. We were inseparable. While Alan was living with me, he went to his girlfriend's house one night. They had gotten into an argument, and Alan pulled out his gun and blew his brains out—right in front of her.

When I first got the call from his mom, I couldn't believe he was gone. He still had a room at my house. I had all of his stuff. This was before the internet, and we still used phone books. I volunteered to call everyone in his address book and tell them the news.

Many years later, an old buddy of mine called me. He told me that his brother had just hung himself inside their mom's garage. When their mom got home and opened the garage, there was her lifeless son.

He asked me to come over, and I got there as quickly as I could. When I arrived, the body was removed, and the cops were on their way out. I held the ladder for my friend as he cut down the rope noose his brother used to hang himself. I remember hugging their mom. It didn't seem real.

What's wild is that years later, I was sitting with my mom in the hospital as she passed, holding her hand. As she took her last breath, I felt the energy transfer through me and then I saw an orange light go out the window.

Color and texture are everywhere—even in death.

TRANSITION

We're still the same people we were 2,000 years ago. We're just not as tough.

Shutdown Workaround

The year after filming *Shear Genius* was a blur. Not only did I witness a drive-by shooting and move to another state, but I also started working with Joico, did Roger Waters' hair (that story's up next, but it comes with a trigger warning for any of the straight dudes who are reading this).

I also opened up a salon in the back of a guitar shop, got shut down, and found a way to keep it open anyway. Got engaged. Bought the house I still live in. Went on the *Today Show* and a bunch of morning news spots. Became a straight-up celebrity.

Everyone wanted me to do their hair. It was nuts.

I was gone for a month and needed to figure out where to work when I got back. I didn't want to work for anyone else since I knew my career was about to blow up.

I remembered that my buddy Jerry had a guitar shop in Griffith, Indiana, called Dynamite Music. There was a junk storage room—maybe 6x10 feet—near the back of the store. It was destroyed, but I needed a place fast since the show was about to air, so Jerry rented it to me for $100 a week.

The bathroom was just a subfloor with a huge crack and a loosely bolted sink and toilet. I begged a plumber friend of mine to install two shampoo chairs and a couple of bowls. That was all I could afford. I got a Comcast digital phone, and for six or seven months, life was non-stop.

My clients had to walk in the front door, past people smoking cigarettes, through a maze of musical instruments, then through a vintage guitar room into a windowless back room with two fluorescent lights, a picture of Ozzy Osbourne, two shampoo chairs, and two bowls. On occasion, drum lessons happened next door. Some kid would be banging on drums while people were getting their hair cut. It was perfect.

But here's where things got tricky … I wasn't technically licensed in Indiana yet. You had to be licensed for six months before opening your own business. As I was trying to keep this shit on the DL, someone ratted me out. But … I didn't find out until I got invited to speak at my old beauty school.

By this time, *Shear Genius* was running, and the school had a giant poster of me on the wall. People were losing their minds. Right as I walked in, I got a call from a 317 number. That's Indianapolis.

I answered. "Hello, this is Ben."

A woman on the line said, "This is so-and-so from the state board of cosmetology. Have you got a second?" This woman had a full-on southern belle Paula Deen accent.

Now, I thought it was my buddy Brad messing with me in the voice of one of the characters he would play when he would prank call me.

Thinking I'm playing along, I go, "Oh, are you? I bet you've got a pretty mouth." I went off—talking shit, being vulgar as hell. I'm sure she was appalled. She probably should have called the police.

When I realized it was actually the state board shutting me down, I nearly shit myself.

I walked into the beauty school, looked at the staff and students, and said, "I just got off the phone with the state board. I thought it was a prank, so I told her all kinds of terrible shit. Turns out, she was real. And now, when I leave here, I have to figure out where the hell I'm going to work because they just shut me down."

Afterward, I called the state board and asked, "What do I have to do? I can't just not work." I considered sneaking clients in through the back door. But when I asked what would happen if I got caught, they said, "We would have to revoke your license."

Damn. I've got to play by the rules.

They told me I needed a licensed Indiana stylist to supervise me for the next three months. The only person I could find was this dude who reminded me of Butt-Head from *Beavis and Butt-Head.* His girlfriend was a biker chick who worked as a nurse for people recovering from sex-change surgeries.

For three months, this guy would hang out and watch me work. I learned a lot about post-op sexual reassignment care. It was so weird. But by the end of that year, I had a crazy client list, and then, right across the street, a bigger space opened up for rent.

So I opened up my first real salon in Griffith. I got busy with product companies, started traveling, and that's when the celebrity hairstylist side really kicked in.

Educating the Educator

Right around the time *Shear Genius* aired, I met Jim Sampagnaro. Jim was a legend—a barber at the old-timer shop near my house by the Illinois state line. He recognized me as the guy from *Shear Genius*. After my haircut, he followed me out of the shop to introduce himself.

Jim owned a company called Educations in Hair. Every other year, the state of Illinois requires cosmetologists to complete continuing education hours to keep their licenses active. Jim was licensed to provide those CEU hours and hosted live hair demos all over the state. He invited me to join him at every show—and I did, for the next 12 years.

He became my Bobby "Slim" James of hair and a father figure to me. He gave me the best advice I've ever received about being an educator: "It doesn't matter how good you are—people just need to feel you."

I got to practice on the biggest stages and in packed conference rooms at random Holiday Inn Expresses across Illinois. Man, I miss Jim. He definitely helped shape the man and educator that I am today.

Adventures in Brand Education

My transition from reality star to brand educator was interesting. I'd met with just two brands: Alberto Culver (Nexxus) and Zotos (Joico). They were the first to reach out to me.

Alberto Culver owned a lot of brands, including Dow bathroom cleaner, and they also owned Nexxus, which was the sponsor of *Shear Genius*. When the show was airing, they were my first meeting. I even talked about my experience on the show at one of their parties at a swanky hotel in Chicago.

They wanted me to go on TV as a celebrity hairstylist and show people how to style their hair like Jennifer Aniston, J.Lo, and other famous faces. But I couldn't wrap my head around it.

I remember saying, "Are people gonna be watching me from all over? I mean, you think women in the Midwest are gonna want to buy beauty products from some tattooed dude who sorta looks like Osama bin Laden?"

I slept on it and talked it over with my badass agent, cowboy Mike, a fellow Hoosier.

A few days before that meeting, Zotos flew me out to their office in Arcadia, California, for dinner and drinks, then I flew back the next afternoon.

While I was still figuring out whether I was going to become a Nexxus superstar, I got a call from Zotos, the big company that owned Joico.

The woman who took me to dinner asked if I'd be okay with going to New York to style Roger Waters' hair from Pink Floyd and an Israeli violinist I'd never heard of.

I said yes. This was a no-brainer for me—not only to meet but also to do the hair of a rock and roll legend. Oh, hell yeah.

My agent let Alberto Culver know I wasn't interested. Zotos won.

Upon my arrival in Manhattan, I was told to enjoy myself at the hotel. I specifically remember them saying, "We have a lot of credits at the Hudson, so feel free to have fun."

Holy shit. I'm in New York and getting paid to be here. This was unreal. I hadn't been to New York since I was a baby.

A few years earlier, I'd done some hair and a bit of no-talk acting for the movie *Transcendence.* I was on set for a few days in Wisconsin, in an abandoned house/slaughterhouse. The lead actor, a cool guy named Andy, lived in New York, so I gave him a call.

"Hey man, you're not gonna believe this, but I'm in your hood staying at the Hudson. I've got a full day off and carte blanche at the hotel. I have to be up at 6 a.m. to do Roger Waters' hair tomorrow. You can hold hairspray and just say you're my assistant."

He was down. So the adventure began …

We kicked things off with dinner on the rooftop. Lychee martinis. Dammit, those things were delicious—and free.

I think I probably had about seven?

Andy knew the subway, so off we went. We ended up at a Japanese restaurant. Not sure if I ate, but I remember switching to sake bombs. Maybe two or three?

I have to think really hard about it, but I vaguely remember being politely asked to leave.

Next stop: a movie release.

No clue how or when we ended up back at the bar at the Hudson. But there we were.

That's when I was invited to a table of people Andy knew. I instantly ordered bottle service, vodka, and tequila for the table I'd just met.

Andy and I—two dudes who barely knew each other from a short gig—raging like over-privileged children at an open bar.

What made it even crazier was that I was getting stopped in the street by *Shear Genius* fans for photos. Wow.

Then, things took a wild turn.

Just a heads-up, the following might be the gayest thing you'll ever read from me.

When I woke up, I was incredibly close to my buddy—like, really close.

Although nothing of a sexual nature happened, it sure as hell looked like it could've.

We were spooning, butt-ass naked, in a tiny hotel room. I was terrified.

My fingers were laced together, just inches away from his frank and beans, but they weren't touching anything they shouldn't.

I am not gay, and neither is Andy. We're both straight as arrows. We just happened to be naked sleepers sharing a dollhouse-sized room.

Here's how it went down:

I was the first to leave the bar. Blackout drunk, I passed out in the hallway.

When I came to, I started banging on a door.

"Let me in, motherfucker! Let me in!"

Apparently, I said that.

Oops, wrong door.

The terrified person inside called security. After my idle threats, I fell asleep in the hallway once again.

Security showed up, checked my ID, and realized I was a guest. Instead of arresting me, they sent a Zeus of a man to pick me up and carry me back to my actual room.

I briefly woke up in the arms of a gigantic Black man carrying me like a baby down the hallway of the hotel.

By the time I got there, drunk, Andy had already returned to sleep it off. When I woke up, I was kickstanding his butt cheeks in a vertical direction.

After some investigation, which included warming up a towel and wiping my junk with it, then smelling it to make sure it didn't smell like shit … then checking the bed and Andy for any signs of physical misconduct (baby batter, etc.), I confirmed no gay activities occurred.

Looking back, I should've gone to the hospital for alcohol poisoning.

I rinsed off, dry heaved in the shower, and got ready for the biggest hair opportunity I'd ever had.

Andy showed up just in time with his can of hairspray, and the most star-studded event I'd ever witnessed kicked off.

Roger Waters, John Mayer, Bon Jovi, Quincy Jones, Mariah Carey, Conan O'Brien, President Bill Clinton, and a whole list of icons were all there.

My assignment was simple: take pictures with a celebrity.

President Bill Clinton, Andy, and Ben at the VH1 Save the Music Gala in New York

Mission accomplished.

After watching Roger Waters perform with a 50-piece children's gospel choir, Andy and I high-fived and parted ways.

The next morning, I was on my way back to Indiana.

Not Great, but Good Enough

Right after *Shear Genius* aired in 2007, I went from cutting hair out of my house to staying in fancy hotels with industry experts.

My first hair show was the America's Beauty Show at the McCormick Center in Chicago, 30 minutes north of where I live and grew up. As I watched the other artists backstage prepping, I realized, *Holy shit—all these other hairdressers are next-level artists.*

I had never looked at hair as fine art until I met Joico's artistic directors at the time, Damien Carney and Sue Pemberton. They were masters of their craft. Their work was the perfect combination of technique and discipline.

At first, I didn't feel like I belonged in this room full of greatness. The only reason I was there was that I was popular at that time in my life, and I knew it. It felt like being part of the cool-kids' club with people from all over the world.

At the show in Chicago, I realized I was a decent hairdresser. I also couldn't move more than two steps without someone taking a photo with me. I thought, *What the hell did I just get myself involved in? Is this how it feels to be famous?*

For the first two years, I worked the major beauty trade shows as a guest artist. Every year, Joico would bring all the artists to California for a hands-on trend training. We learned new cutting and color techniques to use at shows and in classrooms. It was exciting and, at times, intimidating—especially doing it in front of my peers.

At night, we'd sip champagne and dine at the hottest restaurants. It wasn't until years later that I fully understood how massive these beauty companies were and how pro education really worked. They paid me enough money to learn to love it—until I grew to hate it.

FAMILY

A tree without roots is only a log.

Juggling It All

In 2008, I borrowed $50,000 from a bank to open up a salon/clothing store called Bang Bang. It was directly across the street from the guitar shop. My day rate was $1,000 every time I left the house to do anything.

I hired a solid staff and threw myself into everything—hair, photo and video projects, even a fashion show. Did this publicity salon with Pete Wentz from Fall Out Boy that only resulted in two haircuts, but it led to Chicago Fashion Week with him, Ashlee Simpson, the chick from Rock of Love, and Stephen Rosengard from Project Runway. I was making pretty good bank but blowing it all on booze, designer blue jeans, and f'n sundresses.

By 2009, I was everywhere at once—traveling constantly, running salons, doing hair shows, hosting Hair Wars. Still trying to squeeze in recording sessions with my buddy Danny and saxophone gigs whenever I could. Then everything shifted. My dad retired, and my grandma died the very next day. Mom's health was tanking—her skin was turning purple. So I shaved her head with a 4-guard, bleached it out, and colored it bright neon pink. The first time she looked in the mirror, her face lit up. She was so happy.

Ben's dad (Jim), his wife (Angie), Ben holding their son (Marco), and Ben's mom (Gae) at the Chicago Theatre in 2017

She was constantly in and out of the hospital, and instead of people staring and thinking *What's wrong with her*? they'd say, "Wow, you look super cool. I love your hair! That looks so pretty on you. I wish I was brave enough to do that."

One Relationship Ends and Another Begins

I realized super quick that the marriage I got myself into was a horrible idea. I reached out to a mentor of mine named Dov who lives in Israel. His advice for me was to fast. Three and half weeks after my fast, I filed for divorce.

Thirty minutes after I got my separation papers, I drove to a salon in Orland Park, Illinois, to teach a hair class. Angela, the director of education, unlocked the front door, let me in, and gave me a tour of the salon.

After I left, she texted me and asked me about a product I had talked about, and then invited me out for a drink. I said, "If I meet you out for a drink, we'll end up getting married."

Talk about timing.

Five minutes after my ex moved out of our house, Angela pulled in with a suitcase. My sole possessions were a spoon and a cup. There was nothing else in the house. So Angie and I just walked inside and started from zero.

She quit her job a few months later, and we opened a new space right down the street. It was an absolute dump of a place, just trashed to hell. Dead animals, no back door. Nobody wanted it. The town had a revitalization fund, though, so I tapped into it. Getting reimbursed for part of the renovation was awesome. We stayed in that space for eleven years.

By 2011, I still had Bang Bang, but the lease was running out. I started a new LLC called Ben Mollin Hair Education. Took out a line of credit at Home Depot and set up shop. Traveled a ton. Staff was solid. I was winning awards and becoming a great presenter. Taught my first Ben Mollin Project in Louisville.

In 2012, I got married again. The Ben Mollin Hair Education salon was good. We opened up a training academy, partnered with a beauty school, bare bones AF.

Wedding Photo of Angela dressed as the Corpse Bride and Ben as Edward Scissorhands, October 27, 2012

I traveled for Joico and Hair Wars and random events. Was even recognized in *Woman's World* magazine for holiday hair tips.

Started paying back business debt. No music, just an occasional Bobby "Slim" show or fill-in sax stuff with Joe Winters and his band, The Steepwater Band.

Angie and I worked together full time. We were traveling all over the world. We did it all. Bottle service in Vegas. Moonlit dinners in Quebec with interpreters. Sushi in Sydney. It was fucking epic. Magical, in so many ways.

My mom's health was really bad, but she was determined. My dad was starting to change, and his hair and beard were becoming white. The salon was busy, I was always on the go, drinking a shit ton, smoking a lot of weed and missing music. I was making great money, and we were talking about opening a restaurant in the vacant space next to us.

After a hair gig in Tulum, I told Angie we needed to get rid of everything, and move out West. The salon was becoming a major pain in the ass and traveling was getting old. I needed to make a lot of money to keep all the spaces I had and to keep the lifestyle.

Still never thought of ending my life, but I was beginning to question everything. I was booked for over a year in advance. I had become a slave to vanity and gluttony.

In 2013, we opened up Angel Hair Café, a vegan restaurant and juice bar. That cost another $50,000. We had four spaces now. My mom spent a lot of time in the hospital, and my dad's cognitive skills were weird. All I did was hair, beer, weed, food, sleep, travel, solve problems, fire and hire. I was in deep with my career.

Angie wanted to become a foster parent. We started hanging out with a little guy named Chianti. We went through fostering and got pregnant later that year. But not before a shitshow of a fertility test.

Pocketful of Batter

I feel at this point, I need to tell you about my "pocketful of batter experience."

I had a client whose husband was a urologist. Once, while doing her hair, I asked her about having kids and if it was difficult for her and her husband. I mentioned we had been trying for a while with no luck. Within a few days, I found myself in her husband's office.

This guy was a brown-haired version of Ken. After a 30-minute conversation about ball sacks and blood flow, it was time to ram his whole hand up my butt. He gloved up and applied enough KY jelly to pan fry a dolphin. I was then given a cup with a blue lid to crank in. He pointed across the parking lot to a building in which I was to drop off my baby batter.

I hopped on my moped and left for home, made the deposit, put the lid back on, and threw it into the front pocket of my cargo shorts. Minutes later, I was cruising back down the road wearing a Slayer T-shirt, camo shorts from Target, and flip-flops. Just me and my semen, and a 30-minute time limit from blast-off to delivery. Time was ticking.

I walked into the office and stood behind two women with their children in line before me. It was taking some time, but I felt confident that I'd make it. Now it's been about 20 minutes, and it's my turn.

"Hi sir, how can I help you?"

"Hello, I'm here to drop off my semen."

"Your what?"

"My semen."

"Sir, this is a pediatric/family practice; you'll need to go to the lab at the hospital."

Fuck.

I look around, and it's all full-time moms with their kiddos and an elderly African American couple. I can't even begin to explain how that felt. So I took my pocketful of batter and went down the street. By the time I dropped it off at the right place, it had been 32 minutes.

A few days go by, and I receive a phone call with the news that it was possible to get pregnant but not probable, followed by the analogy that "the bus rides fine, but there's just not anybody on it." I went from being determined to humiliated.

We kept trying. A year passed with no positive pregnancy tests. As luck would have it, right when we opened up the vegan restaurant, Angie finds out she's pregnant. Finally.

But now I have a pregnant wife who is working crazy hours.

Marco

On the morning of September 5, 2014, the day of Marco's birth, we go in for a stress test. After monitoring for three hours, it was time to disconnect the device and send us home. That's when his heart stopped.

The heart monitor flatlines, the machine starts beeping, and nurses come running in. Then, about 10 seconds later, the heart rate returns. Fuck. For me, this is when parenting begins.

His heart monitor is beeping more than when it wasn't by a higher percentage. We remain calm and go through every thought you could ever have.

Is he gonna be okay?

Is there a chance of brain damage?

How long has this been going on?

The most beautiful time of my life is now the scariest.

They start preparing Angela for an emergency C-section. Delivery is intense. She loses a ton of blood. This is a very delicate situation that needs critical attention.

They bring Marco over to a table. I can hear him crying. All of a sudden, his eyes open. It feels like I've entered another dimension. This is so beautiful but terrifying.

Eventually, we're all back in our room with our new baby boy.

The next day, a veteran nurse mentions she doesn't feel good about his coloring, so the next step is NICU, which is the intensive care for infants. They take him. Moments later, I wheel my wife through the large open space of the intensive care unit. This was incredibly eye-opening and oddly familiar. The last time I saw the inside of one of these was after the first time I attempted my life at 14.

The nurse says, "I don't know how to tell you this, but we can't figure out how his heart is working."

"I mean, it is, though, right?"

"Yes."

Holy shit. This is when I had to remember to breathe.

"We've called in a pediatric cardiologist to further investigate, and he should be here in a couple of days. Oh, and by the way, his kidneys are on top of each other; it's called 'horseshoe kidneys.' She then draws me a picture of what it looks like, and yes, it resembles a horseshoe. "If he goes into cardiac arrest, we do not have what we need to properly facilitate it, so we'd be airlifting him to Indianapolis for treatment."

The first 48 hours of sleep deprivation are something. Your worry turns into mild hallucinations with just a tad of pure delirium. This was no different.

The hospital kept a room open for us, but we stayed in the NICU. The only high point of the NICU was watching my parents become grandparents. They were beaming with joy. There was something especially amazing about watching my mom—it was purely beautiful.

To make things even more complicated back home, the staff at our salon had just doubled because we acquired six new employees from a salon that recently shut down.

I was stressed the fuck out.

My texts would read, "Hope you, mama, and baby are great. I need to talk to you when you get back."

Fuck. Go away.

No sleep, no certainty on life, and a business I wanted to burn down to the ground.

Two days later, Marco's heart is still beating, which is a good thing. On his fourth day of life, in comes a rather tall Japanese man. It was the pediatric cardiologist. He looks over his ultrasound, and in the calmest and most soothing voice, he tells us that Marco's heart was just upside down and then proceeds to hand-draw us a picture.

"In dextrocardia, the heart is positioned on the right side of the chest instead of the left."

For me to wrap my head around it, I ask if it's kind of like a detour on the expressway when you have to go a little out of the way to get back on.

He smiles and says, "Yes. There is a small hole which will most likely go away. Please bring him back to me in a year."

After the scariest week and a half of my life, we're back at home and our family life had begun. A few days later, I flew out again to New York for work. I was already starting to hate the work I would do when traveling, but this was the first time I felt guilty for being gone.

One of my "bosses" asked, "How's dad life?" I don't remember what I said, but I do remember her response: "Nice not having to change diapers and lose sleep, right?" followed by a slight chuckle.

I wanted to snap back a quick "Fuck.You." but I just smiled. That's when I realized this world I was in was shallow, and I hated it.

The first year of parenting, I never slept. I'd pass out intermittently throughout the night and at times during the day. I was constantly aware of his heart. *Was it going to beat? What would I do if it stopped?* As soon as I woke up, I'd immediately run to his crib and watch him breathe.

A year passed, and we had our return check-up visit. As the doctor did the ultrasound, Angela had her eyes closed, and I don't think I breathed. After the stethoscope was removed and the ultrasound jelly was wiped, the doctor looked at us and said, "His heart is fine, and I never need to see him again."

Angela's knees buckled, and I felt the weight of the world leave my shoulders. Phew. That was an amazingly painful experience but so beautiful. We had a few appointments with a kidney doctor, and after a few years of random tests, we were clear.

My parents had a purpose now. I honestly feel that becoming grandparents kept them alive a lot longer. I had a client who gifted me a piano, and my dad would literally just sit there and play for hours and sing to Marco. My mom had her disabilities, but she was strong. She would change diapers one-handed. Now my parents had something else to do besides doctor appointments and going to the synagogue to keep themselves busy. They could come over to the house to be with Marco. They loved being grandparents.

I traveled a ton and was always cleaning when I got home. It was a very difficult time but a very joyful one. I drank every night. We still had four spaces we were renting. Our salon was the busiest in the area. While I was on the road, Angie was home with the baby.

Angie would bring Marco to work with her. I wanted to get a nanny. Eventually, we hired a manager for the restaurant. I'd had a son, but becoming a dad was not happening.

I was gone all the time doing celebrity shit, but I always felt pressure to get back home—especially since my parents were on the fast decline.

BURNOUT

Try not to die—until you do.

Nonstop for Seven Years

Let me paint you a picture of my life as a "celebrity" hairstylist. I'd fly into town, get a ride straight to the hotel, go to my room, unpack my stuff, and hang up my stage clothes. Depending on my arrival time—and whether or not my flight was delayed—I might get a quick bite to eat. Then, I'd head to model call.

When you work for these hair shows, you need to cast models who are available for one day of prepping the hair and then one or two days to model on stage, depending on the length of the event.

For some of the larger shows, I'd be partnered up with another artist. After we would lock in our models, we would photograph them, and then we'd sit around and figure out a game plan on what we were going to do with their hair.

Model prep was always early AF, followed by two ridiculously long days of selling shampoo on stage inside a convention center. Then off to the bar with the people who hired us and some of the team for dinner and drinks. We'd take pictures and make plans that never happened.

Back home, I'd show up to work by 7:45 or 8:45 a.m., depending on when my first client booked. I'd work straight through to 8:00 p.m. No breaks. No lunch. Just haircut after haircut, color after color, all day long. In between clients, I'd be answering texts or picking up calls—usually from more clients trying to get in.

A few years earlier, my core team had all moved away. One went to Florida, one to Mexico, and one to Ireland. The same year they left, we were voted one of the top 10 salons in Chicago and the best in the region. It looked great on paper, but to me, it felt like someone handed me a backstage pass to a shitshow.

At the salon, I was working 14- to 18-hour days, Tuesday through Saturday, and I was traveling almost every weekend for work. I kept that pace for seven years straight. The money was there. The time was not.

Below is a snapshot of my travel schedule with product companies and the Ben Mollin Project (BMP) for the last two of those seven years. I only know it's the last two because I started running; otherwise, it's page after page of clients and cities and dates for seven consecutive years.

2018

1/14 to 1/17—Dominican Republic DE
1/18 to 1/25—Cabo vacation!
1/26 to 1/29—Long Beach Cosmo
2/3 to 2/6—Joico training
2/7 to 2/8—salon day
2/11 to 2/12—BMP Ontario
2/19—Mariah private BMP
2/25 to 2/26—AZ Gretchen Joico
3/4 to 3/5—Mississippi Joico Kelly
3/9—global entry interview 10am
3/12—Jeremy Houston Joico
3/19 to 3/20—Windsor

3/26 to 3/27—Windsor BMP
4/9—Raleigh, North Carolina Joico
4/13 to 4/17—Richard San Jose Joico
4/20 to 4/23—Montreal Joico Canada
5/5 5/7—Rhode Island Tina Joico
5/14—Houston Jeremy
5/20 to 5/21—Nashville Joico Lindsey
6/3 to 6/4—Orlando Joico
6/11—Asheville, North Carolina Joico
6/18—Richard Denver Joico
6/23 to 6/25—BMP Chicago twisted scissor
7/5—right arm tattooed by Chencho
7/23—private BMP, Los Angeles
7/28 to 7/30—Ft Lauderdale BMP
8/5 to 8/6—Michigan Joico
8/12 to 8/13—private BMP
8/19 to 8/20—BMP Kansas
8/23 to 8/25—Kansas City sales meeting Joico
8/26 to 8/27—private BMP
9/8 to 9/10—Austin, Texas Nicole
9/15 to 9/17—Vancouver Joico Canada
9/23 to 9/24—Detroit
9/28 to 10/1—Cleveland Lindsey Joico
10/6—Austin Greg Lara MC
10/7—Concord Chicago music hall hair banger ball Moline
10/15—Modern Beauty Calgary
10/18 to 10/22—Charlotte Lyndsey Joico
10/26 to 10/28—BMP AZ
11/3 to 11/5—Joico Connecticut

2019

2/2 to 2/4—Indianapolis BMP Private
2/16 to 2/17—Massachusetts BMP Private
2/23 to 2/24—Chicago BMP Tier 1
3/3 to 3/4—Lincoln, IL BMP Tier 1
3/10 to 3/12—IBS New York

3/17 to 3/18—Kansas City BMP Tier 1
3/24 to 3/25—Denver BMP Tier 2
3/30 to 3/31—Chicago ABS
4/13 to 4/14—Yukon Joico Canada
4/28 to 4/29—Cleveland BMP Tier 1
5/12 to 5/13—San Antonio BMP Tier 1
5/19 to 5/20—Fresno, CA BMP Tier 1
7/13—half IRONMAN Muncie
8/19—full IRONMAN Quebec
10/6—last Joico Canada show Quebec
11/2—50k Chicago
12/3—Lakeshore 50/50 (50k) 1st ultra distance
12/10—ran with David Goggins
12/29—50k trail Indiana

My parents wanted to help, but they had their own issues. My mom was handicapped but a friggin' bull when it came to pushing through.

Dad's disabilities were less physical. Without my mom, he would forget to do basic shit like eat or take his meds. He wasn't ever diagnosed, but looking back, he had to be on the spectrum as a musical savant.

All that to say—I had to figure out who was going to watch *them* while they watched Marco.

A caregiver would call with another update. It never ended. It *literally* never ended. Just problem-solution, problem-solution, problem-solution.

The Birth of the Ben Mollin Project

After my run on *Shear Genius* and some time selling hair products on stage, I got a call from this eccentric, cat-loving woman from Michigan who worked with product companies.

"We're doing a new-hire training," she said. "Can you teach these younger hairdressers how to present? You've got this thing about you."

I told her, "I'm good at presenting because I've been on stage—but usually with a guitar in my hands."

Didn't matter.

"We want you," she said. "We'll pay you $3,000."

So yeah, I was in.

But I knew I couldn't just show up and wing it. I called in help—a friend from Second City Improv and a client, Natalie, who coached college kids in speech and debate. They gave me some exercises that they do with their classes to pull from.

I also incorporated a formula called Monroe's Motivated Sequence. It's basically five steps for persuasive speaking: grab attention, name the problem, offer a solution, give a call to action, then sell the benefits. Think Life Alert commercials: Grandma falls down the stairs. Solution is Life Alert. Buy now.

The Ben Mollin Project was born.

My project kicked off in 2011, during one of the most pivotal moments of my career.

That first class in Louisville was where it all started. I made up drills in real time. Had people sing karaoke after lunch just to shake the nerves out. Tossed them into worst-case scenarios to teach them how to think under pressure. Breathed with them. Showed them how to slow down, how to land a sentence like it mattered.

One of my favorites was having them deliver Martin Luther King's "I Have a Dream" speech—full volume, real emotion. It was public speaking meets improv meets full-body therapy.

Between 2011 and 2018, I documented everything in little black notebooks. Filled one, started another. People left evaluations after each class: "That was fun," "Learned some tricks," "You really pushed me."

Which was cool, but surface-level.

What I really wanted was to create a transformation, to make people feel something—to activate them and teach them how to move others. I kept exploring new ways to crack that open.

It took years to create. What started as a two-day class I taught to hairdressers about overcoming the fear of public speaking turned into something deeper.

A mix of creative writing and performance, it was, and still is, a tough class.

One exercise involved identifying three areas of expertise to give a five-minute presentation. I always made people write down three things before sharing an example of my own.

Mine were:

1. Bowling
2. Music
3. Suicide

Then, I'd pick one and begin the exercise. This is when the magic happened. People started writing about personal experiences and overcoming challenges.

For example, one woman said, "I don't know anything else besides hair."

I said, "You mentioned earlier you're a single mom. So you do everything and do it independently without the need of a man. That would definitely be an area of expertise."

She said, "You mean, that counts?"

"Absolutely."

She looked at me for a minute and then just started writing.

When another woman told me she rented a salon suite, I said, "So you run a woman-owned business as a self-made entrepreneur."

"I can say that?"

"You don't have to say it. You already are."

Those are the types of conversations that were leading to breakthroughs with people. It was so much more powerful than just talking about highlights and f'n hairspray.

After one of my projects, a woman wrote in her feedback, "This class completely changed my life."

I called her. "How?"

She said, "You create a safe place for people to be vulnerable. Then you break them down and watch them grow."

I realized that I wasn't just teaching people how to speak. I was helping them become more of themselves—louder, clearer, braver.

I started tweaking how I introduced myself, too. Most start with their name and job title. But what if you lead with your *why*?

Like this: "I'll be known as the hairdresser who changed the way we communicate. Hi, I'm Ben Mollin, founder of the Ben Mollin Project."

After that one shift, people leaned in. And they remembered me.

I posted once on Instagram and booked ten gigs across the country in a matter of days. I made $50k flying Southwest, sleeping on couches, helping people step into the boldest version of themselves.

Since then, it's grown into a three-tiered system that helps people become the most confident, best-spoken version of who they are. I've worked with over 400 people across three countries. The testimonials come from everywhere—Spanish, French, Farsi. Women telling me how they found their voice. Literally and metaphorically.

Now most of my sessions are remote. I coach high-end beauty companies in Beverly Hills on how to pitch better. I work with influencers on how to sell without sounding like they're selling. I tell them, "This industry's just like the music business. Are you punk rock? Are you alt-Christian? Are you selling to moms or rebels? You gotta know your label."

It took seven years to get this system dialed in. Before COVID, this was my full-time job. Now, it's evolved into my life's mission.

The Reality Back Home

In 2017, I did the Ben Mollin Project at a salon in Toronto. Afterward, two of the attendees, Marc and Monika, pulled me aside and said, "We're gonna help you take this to the next level. You've got something." They were salon owners who also worked for Joico.

As the classes got bigger and more frequent, Marc and Monika became part of the project as coaches. Now, I had a team.

That same year, Joico Canada brought me, Marc, and Monika to Cuba to train 50 Canadians to become Key Account Specialists—basically sales assassins. A million-dollar company handed me their top people and said, "Make them lethal." So that's what we did.

To give you some context, a week before the Cuba training, I was working in Florida with my project. I was preparing an educational hair group called The Goonies for a stage presentation they had at the Orlando Convention Center.

A few days before I left, my mom had undergone brain surgery to remove an aneurysm from the back right section of her lower brain, which she had been living with for years. None of us knew.

I talked to her on the phone right before boarding the plane. Her speech was slightly slurred, but she was optimistic and in the process of getting released to go home in a couple of days.

That night, back at the Airbnb with the people I was training, my soul-brother Keon Washington wanted to show me a star that he had purchased for his group. He wanted to share it with me first.

When I asked him why he got a star, he told me that he loved the people he was with, and any time they weren't in the same room and wanted to feel his love, all they had to do was look up. At that exact moment, I received a text message from my wife that said: *Call me, call your brother.*

I got driven back to the hotel, FaceTimed Angie, and then called my brother. My mom was undergoing emergency surgery on her brain.

I took the first flight home in the morning and this is what happened …

Three to four hours into the surgery, my mom came out on a breathing machine with zero brain activity, with tubes coming out of her head. Upon arriving at Rush Hospital in Chicago, I was brought to the intensive care unit where I saw my mom.

The remnants of her pink hair were only somewhat left on the back of her head and behind her ears. The front half of her head was shaved bald, and she had tubes still active, going into her brain to remove fluids. She was nonresponsive and there was a machine that was keeping her alive.

When I asked the doctor what's next, he told me to give it 24 hours. When I asked him why, he said that in his time on this floor, he had witnessed miracles. I asked him what would happen if nothing changed in 24 hours.

He said, "This will be your mom."

Meanwhile, my dad had been admitted to the emergency room for dehydration and a huge spike in his blood sugar levels. I went down to the ER to make sure that he was okay. He appeared to be completely confused and slightly incoherent. I remember having to help him pee once he got admitted to the room. I thought to myself, *Fuck. They're going to die at the same time.*

My dad gets admitted into his own room. Once I made sure my dad was situated, his sister from Indianapolis drove down to keep him company. That night, I slept on the couch in the room with my mom.

I used my mom's phone and called all of her favorite people on speakerphone and put it by her ear to pray for a miracle. I explained to the people I was calling what was happening, and they were happy to talk to my mom and tell her stories and tell her they loved her.

Occasionally it would look like her fingers moved, and her feet would twitch. Every once in a while, it even seemed like her eyes fluttered. Apparently, death has a way of making your muscles move involuntarily.

After 24 hours, the doctor re-entered the room, and I said, "Now what?" He looked at me and said, "If you opt to keep her alive and keep her on the breathing machine, she will then be transferred to Central Illinois, and this will be your mom's life." To me, it was an automatic no-brainer, so after checking with family, we were on the same page.

When I went down to tell my dad that it was time to say his last goodbyes, I wheeled him up to my mom's room and gave him his privacy. I can't even imagine that conversation, but I'm sure it was beautiful.

As I pulled him away from the side of my mom's bed, I knew this was the last time they would ever be in the same room together on this earth.

He looked at me and said, "So this is it, huh?"

"Yep. Sure is, Dad."

After getting him back to his room, I was pulled into the hallway by his doctor. "How long has your dad had cancer?" he asked.

"My dad has cancer?" Fuck.

Apparently, my dad had a rather aggressive form of bladder cancer, which none of us knew about.

The chaplain came into the room and held my hand as I pulled my mom off life support. I took a Superman hat that our son had been wearing since he was a baby and put it over my mom's heart. I held her hand and told her jokes as she passed. Three minutes later, her heart stopped.

I then felt a surge of electricity go through my fingertips, and I saw an orange light once again come up through the room and exit through the window behind me. I felt like her soul had passed through me.

After that, I went back to my dad's room to tell him that it was done, and that his wife of over 40 years was no longer alive. He was in shock. He whispered, "Dead?" I nodded, and he just looked out the window.

It was super heavy. I didn't know what to do. There was no way he could live on his own. He'd be dead in a week.

Who would take care of him? My mom was his brain, and my dad was her arms.

Luckily, at Rush Hospital, they have a social worker whose job is to find care for patients once they were leaving the hospital. I was able to find him a room at an assisted living facility, almost like a hotel-type thing called Symphony of Dyer, which was great because it was only three miles from my house. When I called, they had an open room. I immediately grabbed my dad's credit card and secured that room for the first month, just to make sure everything was solid.

After my dad got situated, I then had to contact the synagogue to which my mom and dad belonged to help organize a memorial service for my mother. We went to the memorial service, and then I took my dad back to his assisted living at Symphony of Dyer, went back home, and the very next day, a car came to pick me up.

I then went to O'Hare Airport; from O'Hare, I traveled to Montreal, and from Montreal, I ended up in Varadero, Cuba. When I got off the plane, everyone else walked through with no problem—except me. I looked like a cross between Fidel Castro and Osama bin Laden wearing an army jacket, and I was the only American on the plane.

I ended up being detained in an isolation room with a woman who looked like she was some sort of probation officer and a gentleman who I guessed was in the army because he had a full-on machine gun.

At that moment, when I was standing in the interrogation room, I looked up to God and simply said, "What?!"

After 10 minutes or so of being questioned, I was on the bus with the rest of my colleagues from Joico Canada, and off we went for a five-day training of the Ben Mollin Project.

In the back of my mind, I was always thinking about home. I'd wonder—did Angie bring my dad over? Did he piss on the couch again? On the books? On the toilet?

With my mom gone and my dad in assisted living, I had fewer people to worry about. But Angie was just starting to pick up a few shifts again at the salon while Marco was at preschool. When I'd get home, I'd immediately start cleaning and solving problems.

Any free moment I had was spent trying to recruit new stylists—renters, commission, whoever—*and* look cool on social media.

Eventually I thought, *How do I limit the amount of problems I deal with every day?* And then it hit me: I know one way. What if I just say, "Fuck it," and don't go back to the salon? What if I quit working for these product companies? What would happen?

If I created this life, I could destroy it, too. Why was I protecting something that was making me f'n miserable?

The last straw for me was in January 2018 at my final show. It was called Destination Education, and it was held in the Dominican Republic. It was an international affair with hairdressers from all over the world.

While my team and I were prepping the models to go onstage, the top dog of our company threw me under the bus in front of everybody there. It was a fucked up power move.

I finally hit my breaking point.

The version of me that I had grown to hate was captured in a photo.

Ben on stage in the Dominican Republic,
January 2018, doing a hair show called "Destination Education"

I was 235 pounds and a high-functioning alcoholic. To put it into perspective, a healthy weight for me is 170–175. I haven't been above 180 since I did my first IRONMAN.

Being a hairdresser for as long as I have, the mirror and I are no strangers. But when I started looking in the mirror after that photo, I *hated* what I saw, *hated* what I stood for, and f'n *hated* what I did for work.

That's when I began planning to end my life.

Suicide (April Fools)

Being alive hurt. Really bad. Before I thought of how I would take my life, I got quiet. Then I became obsessed with end-of-life details.

After my mom's death, I learned a lot about power of attorney and how to access personal information. I started thinking of all the things I wished she would have done to make this process easier. Passwords and banking were on the top of that list.

I got rid of every piece of paper I didn't need to have. This took me about a week. The whole time I was doing this, I was slammed busy with work.

I'm an incredibly organized person, and attention to detail has been the secret to my so-called success, so I made a list and started checking things off, such as:

- Change passwords so they're all the same.
- Sift through bank statements and prepare them for tax time.
- Double check utilities, household expenses, and taxes are paid.
- Put everything on autopay.
- Donate all the clothes that I'm not using.
- Organize the salon.

- Clean everything.
- Set up beneficiaries.

I made sure that all the behind-the-scenes stuff was set up and taken care of. I knew I would be leaving them with a lot of misery, but I didn't want to leave them with a lot of inconvenience.

I can see now that I was lost, I was sick, and I was not in my right mind.

Once I walked out of the salon for the last time on March 31, I wasn't planning to be alive much longer. I announced that I'd no longer be cutting hair and thanked everyone for years of patronage.

I was saying my final goodbye.

That day, after my last appointment on my longest standing customer, I walked away from 20+ years of salon ownership. My celebrity hairdresser thing was dying. My mom was dead, my dad was on his way.

From the comments on the Facebook Live, I read a glimpse of what my obituary would sound like. The options I left for myself were dark but simple: quit my job and end my life.

It was the morning of April 1, 2018.

I was heading out of the house for what I thought would be the last time. I was ready to blow my brains out. But before I walked out the door, I decided to tell my wife I was about to do something stupid. I slipped it into conversation like I was talking about the weather. I thought I was being considerate—firing a warning shot. At that point, my life was in her hands.

We sat at the kitchen table.

And I never went back to work.

The next day, I woke up thinking, *Wait, you mean I'm still alive? Fuck. How did I mess this up? Shit. I gotta start planning this all over again. Damn it.*

To Angie and Marco,

I hate the fact that you had to read this. But I love the fact that I was able to write it. Please know that was then, but this is now. At first, I wasn't going to share any of this with anyone. I felt ashamed. Please know that I am fine. And I no longer have these thoughts.

As we've been working on this book, you'd be amazed how many other people have felt the same way and still do. I want to let people know that everybody struggles at some point. My hope in writing this book is to save as many lives as I can. I love you to the moon and back.

—Me

REINVENTION

"How did you do it?" she asked.
"Do what?"
"How did you walk away from everything?"
"I didn't walk away from everything," I said.
"I f'n ran. If you run away, you get there faster."

—a conversation with Ben F'n Mollin

Getting Honest

April 2, 2018, could easily be the day I was born again. I was afraid, confused, regretful, and nervous AF at first. I started seeing a therapist through a referral from a hair client and dear family friend.

In our first meeting, she asked why I was there. I told her that I didn't want to be alive anymore. She looked at me very kindly and compassionately. It was the first time I ever said it out loud. *Holy shit.*

I went once a week for three sessions. This woman was awesome—total older hippie vibe, and you could tell she was great at what she did.

Our conversations were honest, and I couldn't believe how much lighter I felt than I did before. She told me that she didn't think I was suicidal and said she thought I was a genius.

She's the one that put the word *running* into my mind. She then asked how I felt about having a dream journal, and that's when I quit going.

I went to Kohl's and bought an Adidas sweatsuit and a pair of gym shoes. I thought if I dressed more athletic, I would adapt faster by always being prepared. I was like the K-mart version of Run-DMC or Sporty Spice. And believe me, people noticed.

Aside from swimming in high school from 1988 to 1992, I didn't do much physically until my early 30s, when I got obsessed with Bikram yoga for about a year around 2005–2006. Not long after that, in 2007, I was cast on *Shear Genius*.

From the time I left for LA to film until mid-2018, I didn't exercise at all. I never ran, never went for a super long bike ride, and my swimming days were three decades behind me. By the time I hit 44, I was 235 pounds and a functioning alcoholic.

I hopped on an early '70s girl's Schwinn and rode a lap around the park by my house. The next day, I did it again. My lifestyle of eating out and drinking craft beer stayed the same, but I became constantly active. After a week, I was riding two laps.

Then I started walking around the block. A few days later, I jogged it. Soon, I was jogging to the park, walking/jogging back, and eventually jogging the entire bike loop. I was sore AF. I didn't know the difference between pain and discomfort. My knees, toes, and shins were destroyed, but I realized the pain lessened once I got started. Two weeks in, I was jogging 3.5 miles regularly.

I felt lighter. I had no idea what I was doing, but I felt an urge to keep going. One day, my wife watched a Netflix movie called the *Iron Cowboy* and told me I should watch it too. It was about a guy completing 50 IRONMANs in 50 days across all 50 states. I thought it was a little too much, but it was fun to watch. Up to that point, all I was watching was mixed martial arts, dark comedies, and things that had to do with hair. I had changed my algorithm without realizing it.

The next day, I was lying in bed. I had just quit my job, ended my career, and kept my phone on Do Not Disturb like I was gone from the world (because that was my plan). That's when I stumbled on an IRONMAN video on YouTube. When it finished, the next video in rotation was the Paralympics.

Watching these athletes who were missing legs, arms, and still competing, I broke down. I cried deeply for hours. Something shifted inside of me. Shortly after, I went to Fleet Feet, got fitted for some proper running shoes, and started running more seriously. Three months later, I'd lost 60 pounds and completed a solo half-marathon.

My body was wrecked—cracked heels, a pulled groin, destroyed shins—but I kept running every day. For the first three months, I looked like Forrest Gump before he turned around and started running back.

The weight started coming off fast. I felt myself changing. It's really hard to explain. It was more of a mental thing than physical. I was ready to see something new when I looked in the mirror.

I had been hiding my self-destructive lifestyle with my beard. It was my shield and security blanket. It felt only right for my son Marco to be the one who set me free. I handed him the clippers and watched his face in disbelief as he created a new daddy.

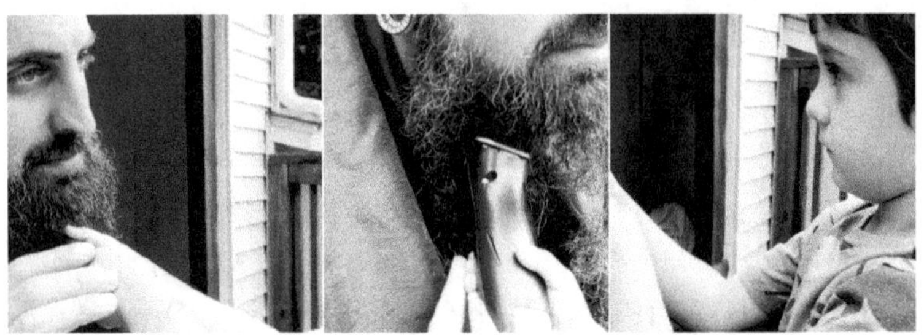

During this time, I was still doing tons of Joico. While working for them in Cincinnati, I got a call from hospice telling me that my dad was near death. I left early the next morning to go to the hospital.

After his surgery to have his bladder removed, he never fully recovered. He just didn't have the cognitive skills to push through rehab. He died in October 2018.

A few days after he passed, I decided to test myself. I ran to the health club, swam 1.2 miles, rode 56 miles on a stationary bike, and then ran back. I did all the qualifications for a half IRONMAN. It took me under 8 hours, and I couldn't believe it.

When I told a friend about it, he bet me $100 that I couldn't do a full IRONMAN. Challenge accepted.

I started to unleash the beast.

Even though I had stopped taking clients at the salon, I was still emceeing for Joico and traveling a ton. By December, I decided to completely deconstruct the celebrity side and build an entirely new identity.

While all of my bosses were together at a Christmas party/sales meeting on December 12, 2018, I drank half a bottle of Jameson and quit Joico via Facebook. I unfollowed everything and everyone.

Then I shut my phone off.

I had officially killed my career.

Becoming IRONMAN

I built a deck on the back of my house so I could cut hair from home and stay home with Marco. I still had some dates on the calendar to fulfill with Joico and my project was still on tour, but I was continuing to lose weight, tear tendons, and break toes. My transformation was underway.

By spring of 2019, I had signed up for IRONMAN Mont-Tremblant in Quebec, one of the most iconic races in North America, giving myself under a year to train. To prepare, I also registered for a half IRONMAN in Muncie, Indiana.

This was a solo mission. I had no coach, no training partners—just me. For me to get to this point, I had to shut off the world around me. I had to ignore self-doubt and pain.

When Marco was in preschool and Angie was working at the salon, Amanda (a theater friend of my dad's) and her mom, Kathy, who used to be a nurse, stepped in to help. They were absolute angels, watching Marco for hours at a time so I could train relentlessly, without interruption. None of it would've been possible without their support.

I'd bike 50 miles, then run nine—sometimes in brutal conditions. At the edge of the pain cave, I would often hear my mom's voice. She'd bring in my dad, and I'd have full-sentence conversations with them like they were right there.

I'd come home destroyed, collapsing on a yoga mat with heat stroke, dehydration, or a pulled muscle. Amanda or Kathy would bring me something to drink and sit with me while I recovered. They watched me transform in real time.

That winter, I bought a Peloton and rode it daily, always following it up with a run. I trained five days a week, with one of those days lasting over six hours. I felt ready enough.

In summer 2019, I completed the Muncie half IRONMAN. A month later, we loaded up the van for Quebec. My long-time friend Mike, his wife (who was also racing), and the Goldstein family joined us at an Airbnb.

The day before the race, we did a practice swim and bike ride. The hills were insane. I'd never biked more than 56 miles, and now I was facing 112 miles of brutal climbs.

The night before, I fell off my bike, landed on my hip, and broke the skin. My wedding ring went into my finger. I had to wrap something around it to stop the bleeding. That night, I couldn't sleep.

The next day, it was game time.

The swim was chaotic—a mosh pit of bodies kicking and jostling for position. I stayed calm and finished the 2.6-mile swim.

Once I got out of the water to make my way over to the biking portion, Angie locked eyes with me and said, "GO!"

Disclaimer: I hate road biking. It makes my privates feel like they are on the verge of extinction.

The climbs were insane, but the descents were even scarier—40 mph downhill. At the halfway mark, I stopped to eat a PB&J and a banana. I couldn't believe I was still on pace.

By the time I finished the 112 miles on my $600 entry-level bike from Trek, wearing a helmet from Target, weight-lifting gloves, and some cotton running socks, my body was wrecked. My left hand was numb, and I couldn't feel anything from the waist down. I had peed on myself without even realizing it.

A volunteer met me at the transition between biking and running and said, "Ben, you can *walk* this marathon portion and still finish, but you have to leave *now*."

I was delirious. I started crying but kept going. At the first corner, I saw Angie and Marco. Angie yelled, "Don't stop moving!"

IRONMAN rules give you 17 hours to finish. At 16 hours and 34 minutes, I crossed the finish line and officially became an IRONMAN.

As soon as I crossed, I collapsed into a wheelchair. My body completely shut down. I couldn't eat. We even debated going to the hospital. Then, out of nowhere, I drank a Sprite, let out a massive burp, and stood up. Somehow, I walked back to the Airbnb.

For three months, I had no feeling in my left pinky and ring finger. I couldn't feel anything from my waist down to my knees.

I wore my medal for a week. Slowly, the feeling returned, and I was able to hold a round brush without dropping it.

Holy shit, I did it.

I AM IRONMAN.

Angie and Ben at the Mont-Tremblant IRONMAN finish-line area in 2019

What would I have missed if I had ended my life on April 1, 2018? To unpack this, I wrote a letter to my deceased parents:

Dearest Mom and Dad,

April 1, 2018, I had a weird day, and I stayed home from work. Funny thing is, mom, I know you saved me and spoke for me to save my life.

That first year staying at home was hard. Really hard, and I had so much pain and anger. I never went back to the salon, and I was imagining what my life would have been if I wasn't here.

To simulate death, I made myself unavailable. I put my phone on Do Not Disturb mode and pretended that I had succeeded. It brought me a very calming sense of peace. The more I became isolated, the more I learned about myself. I learned that I don't like most people and most things. I also learned to become silent.

Mom, it wasn't that I was broken, I was simply out of gas.

July 2018, three months before dad passed, I started walking to kill the time and to kill the bad thoughts when they arose. It's crazy, I figured out that I was emotionally at my worst when I was at home. As soon as I'd step outside and go for a walk, I felt better. It was that simple.

Angie went back to work, and we decided that I'd stay home with Marco. Imagine that! Not only did you never think you'd live to see the day you'd be a grandparent, but I also became a stay home dad! Wow, what an adjustment.

Eventually, I took my phone out of Do Not Disturb. With the money we saved, we were able to build a little studio on the deck, in which I would start to do hair again. When Marco was at Montessori, I'd drop him off and pick him up. While he was at school, I'd do a couple of haircuts, and at this point, I was even jogging.

Sometimes I'd grab Marco and do a haircut when I'd get home, and Marco would sit on a chair, and my clients would just love it. Mom, you would have been so proud of him; he would just sit there and talk and tell stories. I felt like I was reinventing myself through being a parent.

A few days after dad's funeral, I took the day off and went to the health club to see if I could complete the distances to do a 1/2 IRONMAN. Guess what? I was able to! It took me almost 8 hours, but I friggin' did it!

In September 2019 in Mont-Tremblant, Quebec, I completed a 2.6-mile swim, a 112-mile bike ride, and then completed a marathon and became an IRONMAN in front of Angie and Marco. It was one of the greatest moments of my life, and I thank you and dad for guiding me when I wanted to give up.

Who would have known I had it in me? I fucking did it! For the first time ever in my adult life, I was proud of myself. I even got the IRONMAN logo tattooed on my throat to let everyone know.

You know as much as I do, I always went the path of least resistance. This was completely the opposite. It was the hardest thing I'd ever done, but guess what? It didn't kill me. I convinced myself that if I died while trying, I'd die with honor on the battlefield and with dignity—instead of selfishly, like a coward.

When I posted about it on Facebook, I inspired many people. It felt good. Actually, it felt amazing. Marco got to see his dad become an IRONMAN. I was really proud of myself and still am. I became unrecognizable.

When things would start to hurt, I would just think of you and remember all of the things you would do with all you've been through. I thought to myself, *If my mom could walk on broken toes, I can deal with mine*. So thank you for that.

Life didn't suddenly become easier after this, but I am tougher than I used to be.

It hasn't been all rainbows and sunshine since then, but I feel I have purpose. Since you've been gone, I've become a man. Independent of my vices and insecurities. I've taught myself discipline through repetition and sacrifice. I've been telling my story on stages all over the country.

You'd be amazed how many people have attempted to take their lives for one reason or another. You'd also be amazed at how many people can relate to being lost.

There's nothing wrong with me; I just needed to be the one who controlled my misery.

I feel you in spirit and in my mind. Being a parent and a family man has fully allowed me to destroy my superficial existence and live a worthwhile life. I fear nothing and no one except God. I'm confident and committed to constantly grow and evolve.

As my addictions grow less and my curiosity grows more, I find myself completing the circle of life.

We've had some pretty big scares with Marco. He's had several ER visits over the past couple of years. But when I'm faced with a problem, I then focus on the solution. I don't dwell and build a hypothetical world that solely exists in my over-indulgent imagination.

Mom, I've become an ultra runner and a provider for my family. When you passed, I was jealous that you were gone. Now I am so full of life and curiosity that I leave my final days in God's hands. I have found the man I always knew I could be.

I was able to kill the old me and everything that came along with it. In the near future, I'm going to be releasing a book—a memoir about how I deconstructed my old life and built a new one that I don't want to leave.

I'm currently getting licensed in crisis prevention and will be spending my latter years helping others through the darkest of times.

Marco and Angela have grown with me. It's beautiful. I don't get sad anymore, and my tolerance for pain has become insane. It's crazy to think that just when you think your life is over, it hasn't even begun.

—*Benjamin*

Mind Over Matter

I had serious lower back issues from all the shampooing and repetitive tasks I did as a hairdresser, and my feet were trashed. Twenty-five years of standing on hard floors in Chuck Taylors will do that. I used to need arch supports and anti-fatigue mats.

When I first started running, my fitness level was that of a middle-aged, spoiled labrador with a human first name—like Mr. Buckles or Leslie. You know, the kind that gets carried around and eats ice cream cones.

Even standing up straight took effort. I had positional vertigo from years of doing angled bobs—my tall frame forced me to lean over constantly. The curvature of my spine shifted, and my head leaned to the left. Sit-ups made me blackout. I'd feel like throwing up.

My transformation didn't happen overnight. It came from running, walking, biking, swimming … just constant movement. Over time, it all added up to a completely different lifestyle. I realized my chronic pain was disappearing.

Now I can cut hair barefoot without any foot pain. But those first few months of running felt like learning to walk again. It wasn't hard—it was just unfamiliar.

I carved out time I used to spend cleaning, working, or napping, and gave it to movement instead. In the beginning, it was just one hour. But that hour gave me something I'd never had—a chance to get to know myself.

At first, the internal dialogue was brutal. At night, I'd lie in bed thinking, *I'm not gonna drink as much tomorrow.* Then the next night: *Hell, I'm 40. I drink. That's what people do.* That voice wasn't holding me accountable—it just reminded me I was letting myself down.

When I started exercising, the voice shifted: *Dude, you did it yesterday. You're fine. Take a day off. You never ran before. Two workouts this week is better than nothing.*

But I got tired of "better than nothing." I'd been giving 100% to everyone else and settling for scraps when it came to myself. Someone told me if you do something every day for 30 days, it becomes a habit. I got obsessed with that idea.

Eventually I realized: This isn't optional. This is just who I am now.

At first, I used music and podcasts to avoid being in my own head. In three and a half months, I lost 60 pounds. I walked, I ran, then I walked some more. I'd be gone for three hours at a time, carrying water bottles and phone chargers. It became less about distance and more about time—how long could I stay out?

Then I met a guy named Pepi who told me if I really wanted to benefit, I should stop listening to music. That's when I started experiencing everything differently.

In the silence, I started to hear it all—my breath, my feet, the birds, the seasons. Things I'd never noticed because I was always inside, working, solving problems, being broke. I was an indoor cat. And then, like a dog who sees the garage door open, I was gone.

The silence became space for deep thinking. I'd do mental math while running—expenses, income, taxes—and suddenly five or six miles would fly by. But more than that, I met myself for the first time.

Before running, I was just a tradesman. I identified as what I did for a living because I didn't know who I was. My personal life was just an extension of work. Angie was my business partner. We'd get home and immediately start planning for the next day. Put out fires. Wake up. Solve problems. Wash, rinse, repeat.

Twenty-six years of that. Eighty hours a week on the floor. Weekends flying somewhere to be "celebrity guy" for product companies. Then returning to clean up whatever went wrong while I was gone. My brain never got a break—even in bed, the texts would come: *The water heater's broken. Someone called off. The register doesn't balance.*

"Boss" became my identity. No one asked how I was doing. They just brought problems to solve. Eventually, I stopped existing. I was a solution machine.

I assumed love was compromise and disappointment. That business was just survival. That someday it would feel lighter—after a price increase or new hires—but it never did. Twenty years went by.

Success created its own trap. *I'm making six figures without a college degree. What else would I be doing?* The more I accomplished, the higher the walls got. After TV, after all the fame and growth—things only got heavier. I thought I was chasing success, but the process almost killed me.

Now I can say I hated it. Because now I can reflect. Because I made space.

I've spent so much time in silence pursuing this new dream—of doing hard, meaningful things. And here's what I've realized:

When I signed up for an IRONMAN or my first ultra marathon, it wasn't nearly as scary as signing a five-year commercial lease.

Since I started my fitness journey, not once have I thought about killing myself. Have I thought I was going to die? Oh, hell yeah. Multiple times. But the feeling of not dying after a race is euphoric.

Look, I'm not gonna lie. Ultra-running is super hard on your body. Honestly, it might be one of the most challenging things you can do. I have a client who's a cardiologist, and he said, "As long as you keep your heart rate low, you should be fine. You're either going to live to 90, or drop dead at any minute." I thought, *I can live with that. Those odds are okay.*

While running is one of the greatest things you can do for your body, ultrarunning can f'n wreck you if you're not prepared. There's a much higher risk of injury. But if you're smart and preventative, you can train for it. Every time you push that hard, though, it's risk vs. reward. For me, it's worth it.

Crossing these finish lines ranks up there with watching Marco being born. It's that powerful. Except now, I get that euphoric moment without the after-responsibility.

And with this new version of hard, at the end, I want to hear, "Congratulations, man! You did it!" I want to see the look of pride on my kid's face. I want my wife to look at me and know she's married to a beast.

You never know what you're capable of until you silence the voices in your head, stay focused on your goal, and embrace the discomfort of doing something new.

Cross the finish line. Get an award. Go home feeling proud of yourself, knowing you did something very few people are willing to do. Then find the next thing.

Do something hard. Do it for you.

SOBRIETY

If you can't imagine yourself doing something for a couple of hours with someone—without using alcohol—then what are you doing?

Getting Cali-Sober

Oh, sweet alcohol ... dammit, from my very first sip, I was in love. That feeling of kicking back after a long day and cracking a cold one. Going out for a good dinner and a dirty martini—extra dirty. I can honestly say that for a good 27 years, I always had a drink or two on the daily.

I was never a blackout drinker. In fact, I can probably say I've only been blackout drunk a handful of times in my adult life. I was never late for work, never got any DUIs. Alcohol was simply my reward to myself for getting across the finish line of the day.

The first time I attempted quitting was in early 2017. I was drinking more than usual. Parenting, salon ownership, fame, handicapped parents, and a demanding schedule made it easy to want to escape. I always had a drink in my hand when the sun would go down.

On weekends, it wasn't uncommon for me to start drinking with lunch. My mom passed away on June 4, 2017. A week later, I went to Cuba to teach a class with my project. I'd been three months alcohol-free before that trip. While in Cuba, I started drinking again.

In 2021, I decided it was time to pump the brakes. I'd already gotten into endurance training, which led me to take on a challenge called 75 Hard. The app focuses on 75 days of no alcohol and incorporating daily habits to live a more productive and healthy lifestyle. I was two weeks into it when the family and I were heading to Ohio to go camping.

We were meeting Addam who had become a good friend. He lived in New York, and Ohio was the halfway mark. Before he got there, I told him I was attempting 75 Hard. He politely told me that camping with me without drinking was out of the question. That's all I needed to hear, and I assured him I'd continue my alcohol sobriety after the trip. I bought a huge bottle of Proper 12 Irish whiskey and some ginger beer, and we were locked and loaded.

Upon my return to Indiana, I stopped drinking. At first, I relied heavily on NA beer. It wasn't uncommon to drink a six-pack of NA each night during that first week or two. But after that, I started to feel a big difference in my mood and clarity.

Holy shit—did I do it?

I was waking up ready to go. My running became stronger. So did everything around me. Eventually, the need for NA beer went away, and I lasted about two years of being "California sober," which, for me, means zero alcohol, but I'll occasionally use THC or Psilocybin, also known as "magic mushrooms."

Night and Day

When I started doing running events and signed up for IRONMAN, what surprised me most was the community. The supportiveness that you get from absolute strangers completely took me off guard. That, and the fact that all these types of things are day events.

Before I started running, the majority of what I did socially happened at night. When you're in the entertainment business and traveling and networking, everything takes place after dark. When you're going out for drinks or "having a good time" after work, you're not being inspired. You're really just filling a void or maintaining a social obligation.

Seriously, think about it. Conversations—with subtext included—might go something like this ...

"Hey, what are you doing tonight?"

"Oh, I don't know."

"Ya wanna go out and spend 80 bucks and possibly kill ourselves driving on the way home?"

"Yeah, fuck yeah, that sounds awesome."

I mean, it's basically caveman behavior—grunt, chase, repeat. But I think we all do it at some point because it's weirdly accepted. Like, society gives us a free pass to be little Neanderthals for a while.

You would think that I'd wake up and realize what I was doing, but it wasn't long before I started drinking again.

This is what happened ...

With the endurance challenges I signed up for, there was usually—if not always—craft beer at the finish line. I would allow myself one beer to celebrate with the other finishers and volunteers. These beers were different from the ones I drank a few years back. These were *victory* beers—colder, hoppier, and way more magical.

The seed had been replanted.

"I'll only drink when I finish an ultra," is what I decided. The addiction had returned. Fuck.

After two years of total alcohol sobriety, I had two beers after completing a 100k ultramarathon. That "celebration" beer was the seed that woke up my alcoholism. It returned slowly. I'd reward myself with a beer after completing any race I signed up for, and when things got tough, I'd remember that cold, hoppy deliciousness that awaited my tired body and mind at the finish.

For probably a good year, I would only drink at the finish line. The next year, I was incredibly cautious at first and moderated my consumption. I would have one or two beers a week and never kept alcohol in the house. The one beer eventually turned into two. I'd slam the first and be social with the second.

Fast-forward to 2024, and I had returned to social drinking, telling myself I would "enjoy" my summer and pull back the reins a little. Margaritas at Mexican restaurants made a comeback, along with heavy-alcohol-content craft beers.

Granted, I wasn't going as hard as I used to, but it was just a matter of time.

Keep in mind, I was a moderate-to-heavy drinker from age 21 until I was 46. I drank daily, mainly in the evenings after work. Now, at 50, in the best physical and mental shape of my life, I was about to rediscover alcoholism. Damn it.

In 2024, I was still training and putting in long runs, but I started running to breweries as aid stations and running back. Alcohol was now the prize for exercising.

Oh no. Why am I doing this?

I'd realize I was daydreaming about drinking. I was able to fight the urge and not actually consume, but I grew tired of *wanting to.* I started thinking, *You've worked so hard to reach your goals, now enjoy it.*

This same year, I attended an event called Dark Lord Day—an amazing day of death-metal bands and a splendid 14% beer, a true paradise for beer lovers and metal-heads. I scored a VIP pass, which gave me five pours of the Dark Lord. It was delicious.

I called my buddy to meet me later that evening. He rode his bike while I was dropped off at the event, only a few miles from home. On the way out, I purchased four bottles of Dark Lord. I ran while he carried the beers on his bike. I cracked a bottle open and used it as hydration while running, polishing it off in 25 minutes on the way home.

A few weeks later, I got pretty buzzed playing disc golf and ended up buying $80 worth of KFC. The next day, I woke up hungover and couldn't finish my 50k.

That summer, I let my guard down and let the demon back in. I convinced myself that when my son started school, I would give up alcohol once again—but this time forever.

The week before school started, we went to Washington to hang out with family. I allowed myself the freedom to drink. I had just run 70-plus miles, and this was my "recovery." I returned home but this time, I told myself, "I don't drink" instead of "I quit drinking."

Here's how I look at it: If you quit something, it constantly reminds you that you once did it. However, if you don't do something, you just don't do it. At least that's how my crazy mind thinks. I feel healthier and I have more money. Win-win.

What If I Never Quit?

So now that you have some backstory, let's pretend I never stopped drinking. What would my life look like or become? Here's what I think …

The first thing I'd need to figure out is how to pay for it. Getting rid of alcohol allows you to save a tremendous amount of money. I had gotten used to keeping it cheap when dining out, so now there would be a 20% increase at restaurants. I'd have to find ways to make more money to compensate for the alcohol. I'd probably offer one-on-one virtual coaching sessions just to cover the cost.

Since I prefer to eat in an 8-hour window and fast for 16, I would have to start drinking calories before nightfall—making me useless into the evening hours. Eventually, I'd convince myself that a low-calorie liquor like tequila would be the better alternative to avoid the weight gain.

By then, I'd be drinking beer after a long run, and in the evening, I'd start sipping a double-finger pour of añejo tequila which I would eventually start buying and keeping at home. I'd buy two beers at a time—one for me, one for my wife—hoping she wouldn't want hers so I could have both.

After a few weeks of letting alcohol back into my home, I'd start remembering which seasonal craft beers I enjoyed and seek them out. I'd start buying six-packs of seasonal brews I *had* to have. I'd be running my ass off to battle the calories and the bloat.

(Now that I'm thinking about it, my son mentioned that my stomach looked bigger when we returned from Washington.)

With winter approaching, I'd start looking for more tequila to keep at home. At first, I'd make it seem like a special occasion or a reason to celebrate. I'd hide the tequila bottle from plain sight. At night, I'd grab it and either pour a snifter or drink from the bottle.

That's when the guilt and excitement of doing something wrong would kick in.

I'd go out to Mexican restaurants, order a cheap entrée and appetizer, and grab a big-ass margarita. Beer—especially high-alcohol, hoppy ones—would be the norm when I'd go out to eat. And when I got home, to continue the buzz, I'd hit the tequila.

At first, I'd give up THC and tell myself it's either one or the other. But after the newness wore off and getting buzzed became harder, I'd add THC in edible form at night.

This is when the internal suffering would start …

You were doing so good, dude. What happened?

It's okay. You never really had a chance to grieve—now's the time.

Don't feel guilty for being human.

I'd watch myself age faster. My IBS would return. I'd be farting more, waking up every hour to pee. My hydration would be way off, leaving me constantly thirsty and dehydrated. My pants would start to get tight, and I'd be afraid to weigh myself. I'd give up beer and focus just on the hard stuff.

My running would suffer. I'd need company just to get out there, afraid to be alone with my thoughts. My fuse would get shorter. My reactions, sharper. My skin, dry and itchy. I'd grow irritable, unsettled, and obsessed with moving out of state.

Suddenly, intrusive thoughts I used to ignore would be front and center …

Why doesn't my brother ask me how my son's doing?

Am I a horrible husband?

Am I messing up my life?

I'd start looking for open mics—not to play music necessarily, but to socialize, to feel accepted in my return to addiction. Music will always be my ultimate escape from my mind.

Eventually, I wouldn't be able to outrun the calories or the damage I was doing to my mind and body. I'd start getting injuries—due to improper stretching, hydration, and nutrition.

After a few months, I'd be drinking daily. My lust for life would fade. Suddenly, all I'd created to build a full, beautiful life would be in reverse—and I'd be moving toward death.

I'd think about asking for help but would rather suffer silently and hope it goes away.

I would grow sad and frustrated.

I would be killing myself all over again.

Right around my 50th birthday, when I quit for the second time, I had this realization:

If we use the vice we got rid of to celebrate the victory of its defeat, we lose.

In other words, if you lost a bunch of weight and incorporated a healthy routine, would you go out and eat a birthday cake to celebrate?

Would you smoke a cigarette to celebrate one year of being cigarette-free?

If you know that what you're doing in your daily life is shortening your lifespan and altering your mental well-being—are you okay with that?

It's so simple. Not easy, but simple. And we complicate it.

Once I realized the addiction was winning, I decided to get rid of it once and for all.

Fuck you, alcohol. Never again.

I know better now. I want to be proud of myself and practice what I preach.

When people ask my son what his dad was like, I want him to say, "My dad was a beast."

I don't want him to say, "My dad was an alcoholic."

It's that simple.

Beast or alcoholic?

It's a no-brainer.

Beast.

DEATH

You've heard the expression, "What comes next?"
It's death.
Death is what comes after life.
It's how the system of life has worked for years and years and years and years.
And there's something so incredibly tribal and organic about going back to the ground so that something else can grow.

The Final Cut

I'm constantly around death, but there's compassion involved. I don't look at death as something that's completely sad. I believe it's something that's completely necessary. I can't say I'm used to it, but it's always been present.

Recently, I gave someone her final haircut before she dies. I had done her hair for probably 20 years. She's got brain cancer, and she's had it for a while.

The last time I saw her, she was so frail. She was going to visit her grandkids, and I was the last stop before this special occasion. The back of her head was like that of a newborn baby.

I said, "Listen, if it ever gets to a point where you need me to come to your house, you only live 20 minutes away. I'll do it. You're family at this point."

When I got the final text, it said, "Hey, I think this is it." I went to her house knowing this will be her last haircut while she's alive. If her husband wants me to do her hair for the shiva or the funeral, I'll come out for that, too.

I try to create an environment where we're able to tell jokes, laugh, and feel really good. I've learned that I can help prepare them for what's coming—the inevitable. I've had a few clients like this over the years, people I've known so long, I know when they're sick and when the end is near. It's a very intimate experience.

I live for moments like this because it brings so much value to what I do. This is why I chose to stay on this path.

People feel differently when they're close to dying—their hair is thinner, and their skin almost doesn't feel like skin anymore. It's like paper, so fragile that you can barely touch them. But there's this transfer of energy, love, and care that goes into it. They know they can fully relax because you're there to help them look their best.

There's a real beauty in that, you know? We're all close to death. Some of us are just further ahead in line.

The final cuts feel different—like handling an egg from a wild bird—just delicate. You've got to be so gentle. Because their body loses mobility, you can't lean their head into a sink to wash it. You have to spray their hair with a water bottle. Everything's done from wherever they're comfortable—in a chair, on a blanket, even in bed sometimes. You work with what's there.

Angie started doing mobile shampoo services for people in nursing homes last year. She bought a portable shampoo setup so people could get their hair done in bed. She would go into these places where it was practically elder abuse—people with severe disabilities … people without arms or legs—their hair was so matted and filthy. She'd use essential oils to untangle it, take the dryness from around their mouths, smooth out the cracks. It's a really special calling.

Angie realized that the people who needed it most were the ones who couldn't move, so she went mobile. She even made a video with her dad as a model for the setup and started going to nursing homes on a weekly basis.

If you ever feel like your life lacks value or purpose, start giving your time, doing what you normally do, but for someone who really needs it and might not be able to pay for it.

With my clients being older, I'm there for the whole ride. I become part of their lives. I've watched people pass, helped them get ready for that last part. It's beautiful. Such a beautiful thing to share with someone. It changes how you look at life. We're not guaranteed anything, not even tomorrow. We get so caught up in life's obstacles and catastrophes, but life continues. We all go through our struggles. It's not a contest of who has it better or worse.

There's always someone who would give their arm or leg to have your version of worst.

Styling a Corpse

Rob was a supermodel, I think with the Ford agency. He got discovered at a car wash in Glenwood, Illinois, by a top agent. He ended up in magazine ads and did a couple of big cologne ads, maybe for Dolce & Gabbana, I'm not sure. I'd have to dig a little. But he was a cool kid, really into the rave scene—a gorgeous human being.

Rob had a drug problem, though, and he got into some heavy stuff. His sister and I were both a lot younger back then. I was in my early 20s. One night, he went out with the wrong people, ended up in a hotel, and overdosed on heroin. No one called the police—they just took his wallet, robbed him, and left him there.

Two days later, I get a frantic phone call from his sister. She says, "Hey, I hate to put this on you, but Rob died a couple days ago. We're at the morgue, getting ready for his funeral. Is there any way you can do his hair? He doesn't look like himself. His hair's all slicked back, and it makes him look like an old person. It's just not him. Can you do it?"

I said, "If someone picks me up and drives me, I'll do it. Just know that I'm going to have to put myself in a different state of mind because it's going to freak me out." So, I had a glass of Cabernet, smoked a joint to make it more of an experience, and then their friend Marie picked me up. (I still do her hair to this day.)

We went to the funeral parlor in Hammond. The mortician took me downstairs, where it's a big refrigerator—real cold. They wheeled Rob out with a blanket over him. I pulled it off, and there he was, with his hair slicked back and some kind of makeup on. Marie and I just looked at each other, like, holy shit, we're in a room with a dead guy.

We tried to sit him up, but it wasn't happening. If you try to bend a dead body, there's just no give. So, we propped his head up, and when I touched the back of his head, I could feel stitches from ear to ear where they'd done an autopsy. They'd taken everything out, including his brain. He had a scar running from his sternum down to his belly button, stitched up like baseball laces.

So, I figured I wouldn't need to do the back and just started on the front. They had this old-school blow-dryer, something your grandma would have had from Sears—real narrow, with one heat setting. I sprayed his hair down, combed it forward, and gave him that George Clooney Caesar cut that was popular back then. When I blow-dried him, I noticed his skin would change color a bit. Turns out, I was melting some of the makeup. I finished, sprayed it, put the blanket back over him, and left.

When I got home, I took a super hot shower, washed everything. I didn't go to the funeral. I felt I'd done my part.

It was strange because he was young, only a few years younger than me. I'm glad I was able to do it, though. Now, a lot of my clients are older. I do a lot of older women, and if the family reached out to me, I'd go in and prepare them for the afterlife, no question. I feel it's part of my job now, being the last pair of hands on someone at their most vulnerable and innocent moments.

As a good hairdresser with compassion, you have a responsibility. You're there for the highlights of their life and the worst of the worst, the personal and the tragic. Who else are they going to call? They trust you because you're the one they tell everything to. They can have a bad day with you, no makeup on, just be themselves.

Doing somebody younger, though—that was definitely odd.

I think I'd be a lot better doing somebody that was older, for sure, I think it'd be a little bit easier because it just seems more of an evolutionary process as opposed to a tragedy.

You get a different outlook on life. You realize it could end at any moment, and the people you think are larger than life aren't invincible.

Death by Cyber Pirates

Fast-forward to 2021, and Angie brings up a picture from our basement that my dad took of me with my mom, grandma, and younger brother during our trip to Hawaii, probably in 1986. We went for Grandma Elinor's 70th birthday, I believe.

It was awesome, and if I think hard enough, I can still remember most of the trip. It was around Christmas, and I'll never forget Santa coming in on a kayak from the ocean.

Before we left, my mom bought a VCR/camcorder and a tripod. She was filming a sunset when some drunk guys pulled down their pants and said, "Here's your moon." We went to a luau, ate pig and poi, and I even remember buying a conch shell that sounded like a shofar when you blew into it.

After that trip, both my mom and my grandma said when they died, they wanted their ashes spread in the waters of Hawaii.

Growing up, I lived with my mom and dad, my grandparents, and my brother. We never had babysitters—it was always family.

My grandpa was a hustler and a total badass, and my grandma was a legit angel. My grandpa passed away in his 80s—on the toilet, much like Elvis. My grandma was next, passing in an assisted living home the same day my dad retired. She also lived into her 80s.

My mom was next to pass. She was the poster woman for why you shouldn't trust Big Pharma. She was on prednisone for over 30 years, and every side effect led to another prescription. Her pill collection was the size of a small suitcase.

Every joint in her body had been replaced or operated on. Her spine was rebuilt. She was blind in one eye. But I watched this woman move mountains. She never complained about pain or discomfort. I saw her walk on broken toes, come back to life, and run a grade school. She was a beast. She passed in June of 2017.

My dad followed in October of 2018. My dad was amazing. Period. He was the best piano player, and his comprehension of music was savant-like. Anyone who knew him loved him.

My dad was not like the other dads of my friends. At the public pool growing up, there were truck drivers, Ford guys, even a few cartel dads. My dad was the only one walking on his tippy-toes and walking into windows.

I was able to ask my dad's sister, Lynn, "So what was up with my dad?" I always knew there was a disability aspect back then. They'd probably call it autism or savant syndrome. I didn't realize his brilliance until I got much older. Guys that did tough things I always looked up to. It wasn't until I got serious about playing music that I understood I came from a creative genius. He was truly a unique, beautiful soul.

Maybe my story was already written, and the universe was guiding me … I don't know … but after Angie brought up the Hawaii picture and put it in the bathroom, I got an email from

OLAPLEX a few months later. They wanted me to be their guest presenter at a training event—in Hawaii.

I already had my grandma's ashes in a Ziploc baggie in a jewelry box. Now I had my mom's ashes too. I mixed their ashes the day before I left and packed them in my carry on.

Two days before I had to work, I arrived and fulfilled their dying wish. That will always be a highlight of my life as a son and a grandson.

As part of the OLAPLEX training, I took participants to hidden beaches, and we shouted our intentions into the waves. It felt tribal. At a time of chaos and uncertainty in the world, we allowed ourselves to move forward.

On the flight back to Chicago, I edited the video and couldn't believe what had just happened. I had prayed for this, and God had delivered—right on time.

Then, the day I got back, my personal Instagram account was hacked by West African cyber pirates. I had over 10,000 followers. My Instagram was how I got hired. It was my picture book, my video diary, documenting my life as a celebrity stylist and small business owner.

I had always hated social media and still do. I actually blame it for a lot of our problems, both individually and as a society. To put it bluntly, I view it as the devil.

For years, I dreamed of quitting Instagram. I had just fulfilled my mom and grandma's dying wish, and now, suddenly, my online persona was being held hostage. I saw my chance.

When I got the message from a complete stranger acting like a friend who was locked out of their Instagram account, I knew it was spam. I also knew that it was a way to kill my account forever. So I gave them my access code.

Two days after the most meaningful experience of my life, my online self was dead. Holy crap, what did I just do? Honestly, I think it was my mom and grandma setting me free.

Looking back at @benmollin, all I saw was stress—never being home, trying to be "perfect." I hated my fake smile. I hated what I had become. Why would I carry my past with me? How was I supposed to move forward? That first month with no Instagram was weird.

For years, I had posted pictures and videos of my travels. Now what?

And then it all made sense. Now nothing.

That's when I decided to just be. I had no obligation to anyone but myself and my family.

After a few months, I started another Instagram. Since @benmollin was gone, I changed my handle to @benfnmollin. I knew I still needed to be reachable to help others reach their goals and battle their own demons. Today, I only spend about 20 minutes a day creating content and promoting my work.

Now when I meet people, they see the best version of who I am, not who I was. I will never let my professional accomplishments dictate who I am. I will live by my present actions and a "practice what you preach" mentality. The future is unsure for all of us. All I can do is pray for a tomorrow, just to live in the present again.

Almost six years later, do I like what I see? Honestly, sometimes I do. I find that when I look in the mirror now, I can look myself dead in the eyes and not blink.

When I look back at that photo, I see it as a memorial: R.I.P. hair career. R.I.P. salon ownership. R.I.P. Ben Mollin of *Shear Genius* fame.

SURVIVAL

We're the only living creatures that need money to live.
Everything else on Earth gets to live for free.

Life After Death

Does surviving suicide make me an expert?

Short answer: No. It makes me a survivor.

Before 2017, only a handful of people knew my story. I never really talked about it—until someone else did.

Over the years, while cutting hair, clients often shared deeply personal experiences with me. It wasn't uncommon to hear about someone attending a funeral for a loved one lost to suicide.

When they'd say, "I never would have thought (insert name) would do that," I'd immediately start asking questions: "Well, how'd they do it? Did they have a family? What did they do for a living?"

I'd tell them about my best friend Alan, who took his own life when we were in our mid-twenties, and that I, too, was a survivor from my early teen years.

Suddenly, the conversation would shift. I never talked about it unless someone else brought it up, but I noticed that many people had either considered ending their own life or knew someone who had.

The people who knew I was a survivor treated me differently than those who didn't. They listened more.

It's hard to explain, but it was like they were trying to understand me beyond just their hairstylist. Those who had lost loved ones to suicide felt a sense of relief when they talked to me. These conversations were raw, emotional, and meaningful—so different from the usual shop talk.

When I quit doing hair shows and started posting about becoming an IRONMAN, all of a sudden, I started to get requests for public speaking. Up to this point, I had never gotten on a stage without a musical instrument or a pair of scissors in my entire life.

In 2019, I was invited to give a motivational speech at an event in Seattle for one of the largest beauty distributors in North America. I talked about my failed attempt at 14, my mindset on April 1, 2018, my reality TV career, and why I burned it all down.

When I stepped off that stage, something was different. I had just told a room of 400 people that I was a suicide survivor. Everything changed. My identity changed. It felt almost metaphysical.

Instead of people coming up for selfies, they came to share their own stories of survival. They thanked me. They asked for hugs. They *listened*. It was incredible.

During COVID, I did a podcast with my buddy, Joe Chura, on his show *Not Almost There*. We also filmed the episode. He went straight into my attempt at 14 and the journey that followed. It was the first time I shared my story publicly on social media. After that, people started reaching out for advice.

I found it easy to listen and offer support to men, especially middle-aged heterosexual men with families. There were so many of them battling silent struggles. Gay men in the same demographic were also quietly fighting similar battles. (If you're a man reading this, and it's hitting you in the gut—just know you're not alone, brother.)

When it came to women, though, I had to be more mindful. I didn't want to come across sounding like a boyfriend, partner, or dad. I wanted to learn how to be genuinely helpful. That's when I found Crisis Line, a nonprofit.

I went through a two-week program where I was trained on how to handle crisis situations via text. Now, I volunteer when I can—usually at night. It's been eye-opening and rewarding.

My goal is to learn everything I can about suicide prevention. Having a personal story isn't enough. I wanted to truly make a difference, so I put in the work.

Now, I know the stats. I'm learning about the struggles of younger LGBTQ and trans communities. I've learned how to ask the right questions—not to give people answers, but to help them find their own.

Everyone's different. That's what makes us awesome.

I'm on a journey, and when people read this book, I hope to have conversations with many of them about their struggles. My goal is to save as many lives as I can and restore people's faith in themselves. That kind of mission takes training, dedication, and a lot of heart.

This is my life.

And none of this would be happening if I wasn't here.

Navigating the Dark

Recently, I was asked how I avoid going down into a dark place. Man, I live in a dark place. Not a lot of windows and horrible lighting. I've learned how to accept it and make the best of it.

Sickness and death have always surrounded the people close to me. That's been my life, forever.

It's not bad—I'm built for it. In a crisis, I'm the one you want on your side. I don't freak out. I stay calm and make decisions with a clear head.

Bad decisions usually come when you're sad, hungry, or angry—I've learned to wait those out. So now I let things pass. That's how I stay on track.

I'm good with looking at both sides and meeting in the middle. I'm okay with being a straight line.

Here's the thing: We're not guaranteed tomorrow, so why obsess over it? And the past? Fuck it. It's done.

When shit gets overwhelming, I take it day by day. If that's too much, hour by hour. When it gets really intense—like life or death intense—I go minute by minute. Sometimes second by second.

The only way through is to stay present.

When I focus on the future, I get anxious and create all these bullshit expectations. When I look back, that's when depression creeps in. I hate getting stuck in my head with questions like: Am I good enough? Why do I always end up here? What if I'd done things different?

Those thoughts are traps.

Here's something I figured out: Every winter, I make shitty decisions that I pay for in summer. So I stopped making any big decisions between November and March. They always suck.

June rolls around and I'm like, "Why am I in this mess?" Oh yeah—because in February, when it was 10 degrees and dark at 4 p.m., I thought I knew what I wanted. Now I don't plan anything until April. If I go too long without sun, my brain's not right. I've learned to work with it instead of against it.

That was a big shift for me. That and cold-plunging. If you don't have a way to do a cold plunge, just take a cold shower. It's one of the fastest ways to get out of a funk and reset emotionally.

I've always had two sides—a creative side and a destructive side. It's taken me half a century to learn how to balance the two, but I've finally figured out how to work with my brain so I don't self-destruct.

My depressive side would crop up whenever I would hear bad news or have a super shitty day or have a difficult conversation with somebody. Or maybe I was just having one of those days where I didn't see the sun for a couple weeks. The crazy thing is, it's never gone away. It's been there every day. *Every f'n day.*

At some point, it will rear up its f'n little head, and I'll think, *Here we go again,* and then I realize that it's just my brain doing what my brain does.

When I get to that point and don't know what to do, I go for a run. I don't give myself a time that I've got to be back. Sometimes it takes me 10 minutes, sometimes I've got to run 40 miles. Then I come back and I'm better. I'm good again.

Now I'm not as impulsive. But I've had to train myself to produce endorphins—I have to produce so much for it to battle out that depression. For me, running works like a champ, and I recommend it to anybody.

I feel the most alive when I'm challenged. That's why I try to run 100 miles or set these crazy goals like becoming an author or putting out new music as a 50-year-old. I love seeing what I'm capable of.

There has always been a side of me with the ability to destroy everything. But I killed that guy. I'm a huge fan of the guy I am now. He's way cooler and way less of a douchebag.

Pain vs. Discomfort

I've noticed a pattern in my life: take a risk, go all in, and somehow, it pays off. People started wanting me to talk because I'd been through it. I battled depression. I stared death in the face and survived. I went from zero to IRONMAN in 10 months. Now I'm running ultras, pushing limits most people never even consider. I may not be David Goggins, but I've run with the dude.

Goggins is a legend in the world of mental toughness—this badass, "go hard," retired Navy SEAL who redefined what humans are capable of enduring. Meanwhile, I'm over here as a punk rock, tatted, hippie hairdresser who somehow ended up in the same ultramarathon world. We couldn't look more different on paper.

But that's exactly my point. I'm living proof that you don't have to be hard to be badass. You don't need military training or a drill instructor's mentality to achieve extraordinary things. You can be the baddest motherfucker in the room if you want. You just have to look at fear differently. And you have to learn the difference between pain and discomfort.

ULTRAS

"Some people run ultras for sport—simply because they find it fun. Others run because it puts their mind in 'survival mode,' where it's not possible to think about anything else. The voices in their head are silenced. The singular focus becomes digging themselves out of a physical, mental, or spiritual abyss."

—Scott Kummer, race director, podcast host, *Ten Junk Miles*

Cocodona 250

When I bought my first pair of running shoes, I never imagined signing up for a foot race that involved 250 miles across the northern desert of Arizona.

The idea came while I was with my friends Corey and Tony, the hosts of a hairdressing podcast called *Hairdustry*. We were sitting at Go Brewing, which is the non-alcoholic brewery my friend Joe owns. I had microdosed before going out and was drinking "Burn It Down," an NA IPA that Joe named after the podcast we did together during the pandemic.

We were deep in conversation about risk and life goals, and I told them about the Cocodona 250, this insane race I'd been obsessing over since I found it on YouTube. 250 miles from Black Canyon to Flagstaff. Multi-day. Through the fucking desert.

We decided that I should sign up for it. Right there at the bar, I pulled out my phone and started filling out the registration. Corey watched me hesitate over the submit button. My eyes probably gave it away—that mix of pride and pure dread. Then I hit send. We toasted, but I was thinking, *Oh fuck, what did I just do?*

The farthest I'd ever run was 100 miles in the woods. A month after signing up for the 250, I was at the starting line of the Hennepin 100—a race I'd dropped out of at mile 70 the year before. At mile 85 of Hennepin, completely wrecked, I pulled out my phone and emailed the Cocodona race director to change my race from the 250 to the Sedona Canyon 125—the second half of the course.

Cutting the distance in half gave some peace of mind, but I was training during the winter months in the Midwest, so I wasn't exactly prepared for the desert heat and elevation. My buddy Evan agreed to go with me to Arizona to help crew me. This was awesome because he's not only a really good friend but the one who took me on my first trail run. So off we went.

My strategy was to drive to Flagstaff as soon as we landed and climb Mt. Elden. Elden was the highest part of the course, with a peak elevation of 9,600 feet. Our hike went well. I was winded by the thin air but I felt strong. I knew this was going to be the biggest physical challenge I'd ever taken on.

The night before the race, we went out for a huge dinner, went back to the hotel room, and started to prepare. At 7 a.m. Arizona time, I left Jerome towards the starting line. It didn't seem real. When I got there, I already felt a sense of accomplishment—I felt I'd won.

Off I went, jogging when I could and power hiking or walking. At mile six I almost shit my pants. Instead, I went behind a tree in somebody's backyard. Mile 10 was the first aid station. I refilled my water flasks, had some oatmeal and fruit, and was on my way. My running vest weighed around 20 pounds. The distance between aid stations was a little more than a half-marathon.

The sun and elevation were starting to affect me. This was the first time I thought to myself, *I don't think this is gonna happen.*

If I'm having trouble taking a deep breath now, I can only imagine how I'll feel as the distance grows longer. Regardless, I pushed on.

I got lost. Took myself a mile off course. This could've been bad. These areas are incredibly remote—no cell service, limited access roads. But I didn't panic. Stayed calm, used my GPS, got back on track.

The nutrition wasn't agreeing with me at all. I felt like I was going to throw up every time I tried to eat. If I tried to take a deep breath, I'd automatically start coughing. It felt like my head was attached to my body by a string.

At mile 24, I arrived at the next aid station, and I knew I wasn't going to finish. Evan met me there and took off my backpack. He brought me food, hydration, and some jokes and encouragement. Thirty minutes later, I was on my way to Sedona. I felt strong enough but nowhere near good.

I met some dude named Bill. Bill and I were power hiking, taking our time, making small talk. I knew I wasn't going to make it to Flagstaff. Not this time.

At the 36-mile mark, I needed to sit down. This wasn't good. I couldn't hike uphill anymore, but for some reason I could still go down. I decided to close my eyes and rest. It was next-level exhaustion—probably dehydration mixed with heat stroke.

I thought about my family—Marco, Angie, my mom and dad. *Can I do it? I don't know, maybe. But am I going to do it?* I called Evan to come pick me up.

Walking down, I came across a runner who was doing the 250. He says to me, "How are you gonna feel tomorrow if you quit right now?"

"Man, that's a good question. Like shit."

I should get to Sedona. He gave me a gel pack and told me to eat it. It helped, but I still felt like shit. When I lay down, I wasn't sure if I was going to lose consciousness. I felt myself going down a dark tunnel. This time, the dark tunnel wasn't a bad place. It was familiar. I questioned myself: *Is this a good idea or a bad idea?*

I didn't have enough gas in the tank to complete the original 125 miles. But I didn't want to tap out at some random tree with ants on my legs, four miles from an aid station. So I went forward. Those four miles to Sedona were the hardest four miles I've ever done—and the most beautiful.

I did it. I showed up. When I got to Sedona, I passed out and slept for almost five hours. When I woke up, I felt better. To continue, I would've had to go 17 miles and climb over 4,000 feet in the middle of the night. If I experienced the same thing I did at mile 36, I'd be putting myself in real danger.

In the past, when I couldn't finish an event, it destroyed me. I'd think about it day in and day out. This was different.

The sense of accomplishment I felt making it from Jerome to Sedona was unreal. The fact that I didn't finish something next to impossible didn't bother me at all. Instead, it unlocked something in me. I was proud of myself.

Pacing a Legend

I f'n love the sport of ultrarunning. I love everything about it.

I can't stress enough how awesome the ultrarunning community is. I belong to a few Facebook groups, and one of them is dedicated to the Hennepin 100, the race I tapped out of in 2022 at mile 72 and went back to finish the next year.

So I see this post from a guy named Henry Bickerstaff from Oklahoma, and he's looking for a pacer. (A pacer is a runner who assists another runner on the back half of a race when they've signed up for the full distance). Henry wants someone to pace him from mile 47 to the finish line.

Let's do the math on that—that's a little over two back-to-back marathons, through the night, with no sleep and no extended stops. I'm intrigued.

I click on his profile—and that's when I know I'm in.

Henry is 70 years old and the 66th inductee into the Oklahoma Accounting Hall of Fame. His profile pics show him completing the rim-to-rim-to-rim (R2R2R) challenge of the Grand Canyon and finishing Western States, the legendary mountain race through Northern California.

I accepted. It felt random and rare—a unique opportunity I couldn't pass up. So I started training.

Before the race, I got a few emails from Henry—detailed, super-pro spreadsheets with time projections and GPS coordinates. He was prepared, and so was I.

I headed to Aid Station 10 of the Hennepin 100, where I'd meet him.

Weather in the Midwest is tricky, to say the least, and it was super hot for early October. I had my tracker on him, and in about 11 hours, he called me for the first time. Prior to this, we had never spoken. He said he would be there in about 30 minutes, and I said, "Let's go!"

When he arrived, I grabbed his drop bag, he grabbed what he needed from it, slipped me some cash, and we hit the trail.

The first couple of miles, we started talking. We talked about our families and shared stories. I told him that I'd never run with a Hall of Famer, and he asked me about my tattoos.

I told him that some people collect trinkets or figurines. I collect tattoos. He seemed satisfied with that.

We kept it light and focused on one thing, and that was the finish line.

We walked at a quick pace for two minutes and then ran for eight minutes. I stayed a few feet in front when we weren't talking. At the 53-mile mark, it started to get dark.

Running through the night is quite possibly the hardest and greatest feeling in the world. Everything looks and feels different. The temperature drops, and so does the light. You are alone with only a headlamp and your will to push. Walking or running from sunset to sunrise will change your life.

As the dark settled in, it felt like we were going to work. We had learned earlier we both loved Zeppelin. We ran in silence for hours. With 30 miles to go, we switched to two minutes running, two minutes walking. Henry knew exactly what he was doing. My job was to help make sure he did it. And he did.

We only stopped at aid stations to hydrate—quick in, quick out. We fueled and kept moving. I started blasting Led Zeppelin from my speaker. I danced. I played air drums. I screamed the lyrics.

At night, I stayed a few feet in front of Henry. When we walked, I kept a fair distance in front. We had an unwritten law we were following. We didn't need to speak; we just understood what we needed to do, and that was that.

I respected him from the start, and I felt the same in return.

The part of the race I'll never forget is when he started throwing up while walking and running. We stayed calm, and we were able to get his stomach back a little bit as the vomiting subsided. He never stopped moving! At this point, I realized I was running with a beast. It was the most badass thing I've ever witnessed.

The sun started to rise, and we ran through it. Henry said to me, "Can you take a picture of me with the sun rising behind me?"

I pulled my GoPro out and captured it all.

As the sun came back out, we kept moving. Some of our running was at a 10:30 pace. We were getting faster toward the finish. I felt stronger than I ever have. Never once did I experience any discomfort during this whole race. I was on a mission, and this race had a purpose beyond my own glory and grit. I was too busy wanting someone else to reach a goal. I love that.

Henry crossed the finish line in 25 hours and 12 minutes, making him the current 2024 leader for 100 milers in the 70-plus age division in North America.

Ben Mollin with Henry Bickerstaff at the finish line of the Hennepin 100

After he finished, I took a few photos, grabbed a vegan burrito and a brownie, and hit the road.

Thirty minutes into the drive, I pulled over for a 15-minute nap. When I got home, I unpacked, took a hot/cold shower, and went to a birthday party for one of the kiddos at my son's martial arts studio. It was awesome. I ate homemade Mexican food until I couldn't breathe.

There's no such thing as coincidences in my world.

Sometimes, we just get to do epic shit.

And this was f'n epic.

Sedona Canyon 125

When I came home from the Sedona Canyon 125 last year at mile 40, I was broken, but I also learned a lot about the event and about myself. The following year, I decided to go back—alone. This time, it was personal.

I started working with a trainer named Chris Putrich in January 2025. After 40,000 feet of vertical gain on a treadmill and over 1,000 miles of distance, I had a much better understanding of how to run across a rugged, high-elevation trail system in northern Arizona.

When I showed up at the starting line this year on May 9, 2025, I was ready. Once the race started, little did I know, it would be one of the most profound spiritual experiences of my entire life.

This time, when I hit mile 40, and I felt really exhausted, I just kind of sat there, gave myself a minute, and reconnected. The next thing I knew, I'm leading a wolfpack into the unknown.

I felt guided. It's the only way to explain it. God was with me the whole entire time. It's like I had protection with me, and I was invincible. I didn't stop. For 56 hours, I didn't sleep—except for maybe an hour and a half, which I'd never done. And when I crossed that finish line, I still had gas in the tank.

It was cool going out there alone and just allowing myself to be guided. There's so much to unpack. It's weird, but my first week home, it didn't even feel like I did it. If I hadn't stepped on my kid's toy—some piece of shit plastic that we probably bought off Amazon for $20—I would be free from injury.

My legs didn't hurt. My knees were fine. I could bend. I was untouched.

Then I went to brush my teeth. When I looked down, my foot was covered in blood. I'd stepped on my kid's toy. Of all the things to step on—you've gotta be fucking kidding me.

So there I was, fresh off this surreal experience, and instead of going for a jog, I had to get surgical glue to keep my foot from bleeding out.

The plastic monster toy that Ben stepped on after the race.

Ok, back to the race. I fly out to Arizona and stay the first night with Angie's family in their gorgeous home overlooking the mountains. Angie's aunt is cooking chicken while I'm cutting her husband's hair, and then their daughters come home.

We're all sitting together at the dinner table, talking and laughing. It was magical. I slept downstairs in my own little villa, woke up, had coffee, and went to her chiropractor appointment. The chiropractor that she goes to is the same as Tom Brady's. Just random shit.

It's time to leave, so I get a Lyft to the registration station. The driver is this Mexican dude from the West Coast who likes Chicago house music from the 1990s. So we just jam house music the whole way up there.

I get checked into a motel in Cottonwood called the Iron Horse. Across the street is an Italian place that I had been eyeing every time I went out there. I order the carbonara, which ends up being one of the best meals I've ever had in my life as far as pasta goes. I walk back to the motel and spend the rest of the evening anxiously packing.

I wake up the next morning thinking my Lyft will show up, but it never does. I figure I'll hitchhike by standing in the center of the road in hopes that a runner will stop to pick me up. I'm sure they would've, because there are so many great people in the ultra community. I hitch a ride with this couple going up there for the start line, and that's when the kindness of strangers begins.

We all line up at the beginning of the race. After the gun goes off, it's time to go. I start walking it. The year before, I took off running, but not this time. Right around mile one, a guy beside me named Chris starts some small talk.

I say, "Last year I went out too early, blew my load by mile 40. But this year I've been working with a coach, and I'm gonna get it done."

He says, "I've been working with a coach too. I'm obsessed with this race. I've never run more than 50 miles, but you seem like somebody that might be a good person for me to try to keep up with."

I ask, "What's your story?"

"I'm ex-Navy. I was a medic."

"No shit. How are you with navigation skills?"

"Good."

"You point me in the right direction, I'll get you to Flagstaff."

"You got a deal."

We pinky swore, and we fucking did it. He kept me on course, and I ran with him to Flagstaff, where his whole family was waiting for him—including his daughter and two sets of grandparents. His brother-in-law even ended up pacing us for a little bit.

Later, in Sedona, we picked up a guy named Jeff, but after a while, his stomach took a turn. Randomly, Jeff would have violent bouts of diarrhea and then catch back up with us. Another guy named Jim joined us, but Jim eventually fell behind and needed to sleep it off.

Then Jeff went to go take another violent shit and threw his pants over a cactus. When he put his pants back on, he got himself in the fucking cock and balls with cactus needles and then had to comb them out, but he combed them out after running with them for 10 miles. Damn.

At night, we had to go up the side of rock mountains. I mean, one wrong move and you're done. Doing stuff that would be difficult during the day, but in pitch blackness with just a headlamp on, it's terrifying.

We were in the middle of a mountain system with nothing around us. There were a couple runners in front of us, and one of them started panicking. We could hear her saying, "I can't do it. I don't wanna die! Help!" That level of fear is intense.

Whenever we'd have to sleep, we'd just stop, close our eyes, and lie down right on the dirt. That would give us a recharge. Then we'd stand back up and keep going.

With the sleep deprivation, I would see orbs and pink and orange rays of light. The hallucinations were completely real. I believe I was seeing spirits because we were on ancient land.

It was the most spiritual thing I have ever done. Ever.

As I was running, I kept thinking about the difference between hearing "Congratulations!" at the end of the race instead of "What happened?" and all this other shit that I talk about. I thought, *It's time for you to cash that check—to do the thing you've dreamed of and trained for—to kill the thing that almost killed you.*

I had a violent nosebleed. I was dehydrated. I thought I was gonna pass out. I didn't have enough water for a 19-mile section in Arizona 90-degree heat. I mean, everything was set up to destroy me, but I was able to march through it.

In my last mile, I barely even remember calling some of my close friends and family.

As I was running to the finish line, I started crying. I cried hysterically, the same way I did when I was watching those Paralympics when I was at my transition stage. I couldn't stop.

I was given 75 hours to get the belt buckle, and I did it in 56. I finished 108 out of 260 people—90 people didn't even complete the race. It's just mind-blowing. I still can't believe it happened.

The afternoon that I finished, I sat at a table with the wolfpack and their families. Before coming home, I stayed in a cheap, shitty motel, right on Route 66. I literally had to wear flip-flops in the shower and double lock the doors.

With the time and terrain available to me, I found a way to conquer the northern mountains of Arizona for a grand total of 130 grueling miles. Absolutely f'n nuts.

This is for everybody that's been chopped down at the knees. People who are out there busting their ass, fucking killing themselves to make ends meet. I want them to read this and think, "Well, if he could do it, I could do it."

I just got used to doing hard things. At first it sucked, but eventually it didn't suck anymore, and I could push a little further.

Of course, I've asked myself, *Why was I able to do it at 50 and not 49?* And, *What's the difference between me on May 9th, 2024, and May 9th, 2025?* If you watch the videos from both races, you'll see the same person—but an entirely different mindset. The first attempt almost destroyed me. But I came back the next year knowing what to expect.

Conquering the Sedona Canyon 125 made me realize that I can do anything I set my mind to. The course was basically the same, but I came back prepared—and a lot tougher than I was the first time. Last year, I was trying to look cool on social media. This time, I was out there by myself, talking to God.

I listened to music for maybe 45 minutes and then realized I had to shut it off because it was too much of a distraction. I put my cell phone on airplane mode and became unreachable. When I would turn it on, I would just let people know, "Hey, I'm still going."

I knew when people were going to bed, they were waking up thinking, *Let's see if my boy's still doing it.* When I started getting their text messages, that's when the tears started.

They said, "You have no idea how amazing this is to watch."

I would text back, "You have no idea how much this means to me. I'm doing it. I'm going to fucking do it."

Ben crossing the finish line of the Sedona Canyon 125 on May 9, 2025

When I hit the 125-mile mark, knowing that I was 20 hours ahead of schedule, I couldn't believe it. I was unscathed. I was walking fine. I was sitting fine. Not one issue. Nothing. My stomach never bogged. I never tapped out at an aid station. It was perfect. I honestly feel it's because of the intention I set before I left: to have a conversation with God.

The race showed me that I've grown. I've matured. Everything about this sport finally makes sense to me now. I don't need to prove anything else—this race was my mountaintop.

Going forward, I'll still be part of the ultrarunning community, but more as a volunteer and pacer helping others reach their goals.

For me, this wasn't a race—it was a spiritual awakening. My life has just begun.

LESSONS

"Be hard to kill, easy to love, and ready to lead."

—Jose Guitierrez

My Heroes Wear Capes

After losing my mom at 64 and my dad at 70, I started thinking a lot more about my future—how I wanted to age, how I wanted to feel. I stopped caring about how people got rich. I started asking my older clients—people over 70—about *health.* You can have all the money in the world—but if you lose your health, none of it matters.

Now I look to totally different role models—older people who look good—people with no aches and pains. I'm not asking high-level business owners about pricing strategies anymore. I'm asking my clients while they're sitting in my chair, "How are you still hot at 70? What do you use on your skin? Do you stretch? How much water do you drink?"

These are people who weren't used to being asked those questions—and they love sharing. And I love learning. That's how the next chapter of my life began.

Minimalism = Freedom

When our furnace started dying, I needed $5,000 to get a new one. Instead of dipping into savings, I decided to sell the Cartier watch that I bought while bourbon-drunk in a jewelry store.

I looked at this expensive time piece sitting on its ridiculous winder and thought, *The only people who ever notice when I wear it are assholes. This thing is either going to get me compliments from people I don't like or keep my ass warm.*

So I traded it in for a furnace. I use the furnace more often. It comes in handy.

Why I Run

So I never have to lose weight again
To show my son I can
To feel better than I did
To clear my mind
To get outside
To be called an ultra runner
To shop for shoes
To be an active part of the lifestyle
Because I don't enjoy being pissed off
It eliminates overreacting in stressful times
To learn myself
To meditate
To feel the earth
Because I'm blessed enough to have two legs that can
To inspire others
To test my limits
For respect
To be at peace
To identify as being a warrior
To control my life

My Top 10 Lessons Learned as a Salon Owner

In no particular order, these are the top 10 lessons I've learned from owning beauty salons and doing hair for over 30 years. Some are mistakes I either wish I had made sooner or could have avoided in my professional career:

10 | Keep your overhead low but your talent high. I never had a salon that lost money or couldn't repay a debt. I'd set up salons in the backs of stores, buy tool boxes, and hire my friends. I learned a long time ago that people need clean bathrooms, their name remembered, coffee, and a damn fine haircut. They don't need fountains and all that shit—especially the cool ones.

9 | Treat my color inventory closet like cocaine deals in the cartel. Everything weighs out in ounces and grams. The less you spend, the more you can make. Never flush your money down the sink. Measure everything like a bar does—have a digital scale. It keeps everyone honest and intentional.

8 | Do not have sex with anyone that you work with. Drama from the inside will destroy the salon. However, when you're outside of the salon, do whatever you want. No one has any control over that nor should they ever cross that line. Show up, create a safe space, and do top-notch work. Have fun, but don't fuck it up.

7 | Always play good music. You should never hear a commercial at the salon.

6 | Lock everything up that you don't want taken. Toilet paper will disappear, stuff on shelves randomly moved, color tubes, shampoo, clips, etc. Make it airtight.

5 | Pay more for better help. I'd rather have one person with common sense and initiative than two fuckers that'll just stand there and need to be told what to do and then do a shitty job.

4 | Embrace technology and always be current. Just because you think something sucks doesn't mean that it does. It just means you don't do it. The more people you can reach consistently, the better chance for financial success and growth.

3 | Don't throw a Christmas party. Ever. Total waste of time and money. You see those fuckers more than your family. Give 'em $100 cash and whatever they drink and they'll love you forever. Keep it simple.

2 | Invest in good security. Lots of cash flying around on busy days. Salons are easy targets to get robbed. Get a gun. Bad guys are always around. Keep it safe and fun. Women need safety to truly relax.

1 | Don't start a salon. Go find a cool job. Find your people. Do hair in your basement, your friend's house, or out of your van. That's what's cool about it. Never think you have to have a business to become someone. They're just businesses. They cost a lot of money and at times can bring you great financial happiness and at other times the feeling of loss. You can do cool shit with cool people and still become a millionaire.

A Love Letter to Hairdressers

The first time we look in the mirror and share a smile back, we begin to understand the word "love."

We become good at reading faces.

We are with them at the greatest and most horrific parts of life.

"I'm going to be a grandmother," she says. "I want to look my best for the baby shower."

"I don't know how I can live my life without him. I'm still in shock he's gone."

We listen, we laugh, we cry.

We offer advice and lend an ear and our heart.

We touch people …

They trust us …

We begin to understand the word "love."

Life Lessons for Artists

I think I've had almost every imaginable conversation you can have with another human being. And what I've noticed after talking to hundreds of thousands of people from all over the world and all walks of life is that we're *all* fucked up. All of us. Even people who seem like they've got all their shit together.

Everyone has some level of crazy. It's the one thing we all have in common: we're all f'n nuts. And we're all just winging it. We all have the same struggles, the same obstacles, the same hopes and fears.

If you feel like a hot mess and want to know why, check out the usage section of your phone. I only recently started monitoring my screen time. I noticed that when I felt anxious or short-fused, my phone was usually the culprit.

Unfollowing everyone on social media has helped me tremendously. Social media has made us all insane in so many unique ways we'll never admit to.

Limiting social media, becoming organized, and getting disciplined took a long time to figure out in the beginning, but it saved my life.

As a creator, if you're not allowing yourself the time and space to create, you're dying. If you're an artist, be an artist. Create. See what you can do. Share it. Otherwise, you're already dead.

Life Lessons for Marco

Don't tell anyone what you're up to when you're chasing a dream.

Only share what you're doing when people ask. The ones that ask are either supportive or jealous.

First create the memory for you and only you. Then tell your story to those who will listen.

Never waste your breath.

Only apologize if you did something wrong.

We have no control over what is going to happen in life, only how we respond.

Momentum is a state of mind.

Protect your body early on against wear and tear. It's one less thing you've got to worry about as you get older.

Don't tell anyone your goal is success. They'll know once you get there.

You're never guaranteed tomorrow.

Telling people you're going to start something only makes you a talker. Be a doer.

Your actions will speak louder than your words.

Never be afraid to admit to yourself that you are wrong.

Women are into people and guys are into things.

Men fall in love with the idea of relationships.

Women actually fall in love. Never forget that.

At times, life will not make any sense. This is normal for everyone, so stay calm.

Never yell at your problem. It only makes it bigger.

Discover what you need instead of what you want.

Necessity is the answer to being free.

Desire will be the death of common sense.

Shake a guy's hands like you mean it.

And for fuck's sake, make good eye contact.

"Please" and "thank you" go a long way.

Never be a dick.

Good decisions lead to a good life. Bad decisions lead to a bad life.

Find balance and walk the line.

And if you still live in Indiana and you're reading this, do yourself the favor of moving. I'm 50 and hopefully this book is one step closer to breaking the generational curse of living in the Midwest. We belong in the mountains.

Life Lessons from My Parents

My parents were amazing. Loving. Steady. My mom, even with all her surgeries and health stuff, was always upbeat. My dad, same. You could wake him up at 4 a.m. and he'd crack the same jokes. It was almost spooky how repetitive they were. But comforting, too.

I was raised in a house with no judgment. Just love. I was never told I couldn't do something if I wanted to try. Not once.

The only person who ever gave me shit for going to beauty school was my grandpa—who, by the way, used to run a drugstore and was in the mob. He gave me this look and said, "Beauty school?"

And I came back with, "What do you mean?" That was it. Never mentioned it again.

My parents were all in. "You want to go? We'll pay for it. Let us know what you need." That's how they were.

And even when they caught me with a bunch of weed, I said, "Hey Mom, instead of working this out, I'm just going to move in with my buddy Quent and sleep in his garage."

She said, “Okay, if it doesn’t work out, just come home.” No drama. No lecture. Just love and trust.

I’ve never felt that pressure of trying to live up to someone else’s standards. Never wondered if I was disappointing them. I don’t even know what that feels like. And that might sound crazy, but it’s the truth.

That’s how I raise my son—no judgment. If Marco wants to play chess, great. If not, also great. I’m just there to support him. He’s not here to fulfill my expectations—he’s here to be his own person. Not everybody thinks that way, but they should. And if they don’t, I’m ready to fight them. Send them over—I’ll kick their ass.

What’s funny about that is to this day, I’ve never been in a fistfight. But a group of us kids used to do backyard fight club matches—bare-knuckle. We called it Fugazi. The only rule: no face shots. So yeah, I’ve fought, and if I had to, I could unload a bucket of whoop-ass.

Life Lessons from Parenting

Life is simple. We’re the ones who complicate it with all our expectations and rules and bullshit. Marco told me two years ago he wanted to be a mailman. I told him he’d be the best damn mailman in the world. I asked if he’d bring my mail to my house, and he said yeah. I said, “Man, I’d be so excited to get mail from you.”

If he’s 18 and tells me he wants to make sandwiches at a casino, I’d be like, “What shift are you working? I’ll be there every day. You’d make the best damn sandwich I’ve ever had.” And I’d mean it. I might cry just saying that out loud.

He can do anything. All I ask is that he follows the same two rules my mom gave me: don't be a dick, and don't do a drug you're not willing to share or tell your mom about. That's it. If he follows those two, he can live however he wants. I'll back him up all the way.

Same goes for anyone I care about. When Angie wanted to become a sound therapist? Great idea. She wants to make cosmetics? Awesome. My first thought isn't *How much will that cost?* or *Are you going to make money?* It's, *How can I help?*

You want to do something that brings you joy and doesn't hurt anybody? Then go. Go all in. Be a mailman. Make sandwiches. Start a record label. I don't care what it is.

No limits. No bullshit.

Just be real. Be consistent. Be you.

THE FINISH LINE

It's hard to believe that seven years ago, I was ready to end my life. I had reached my professional goals, but it was all bullshit.

Preparing for my own death allowed me to rid myself of everything that was killing me. If you have the ability to do all the planning, then go one step further before you pull the trigger. Open your mouth and tell someone how you feel. Just have an honest conversation about it.

I opened with the Desiderata, and I want to close with it. These words are so important to me that I have them tattooed on my back.

Desiderata

Go placidly amid the noise and the haste, and remember what peace there may be in silence. As far as possible, without surrender, be on good terms with all persons.

Speak your truth quietly and clearly; and listen to others, even to the dull and the ignorant; they too have their story.

Avoid loud and aggressive persons; they are vexatious to the spirit. If you compare yourself with others, you may become vain or bitter, for there will always be greater and lesser persons than yourself.

Enjoy your achievements as well as your plans. Keep interested in your own career, however humble; it is a real possession in the changing fortunes of time.

Exercise caution in your business affairs, for the world is full of trickery. But let this not blind you to what virtue there is; many persons strive for high ideals, and everywhere life is full of heroism.

Be yourself. Especially do not feign affection. Neither be cynical about love; for in the face of all aridity and disenchantment, it is as perennial as the grass.

Take kindly the counsel of the years, gracefully surrendering the things of youth.

Nurture strength of spirit to shield you in sudden misfortune. But do not distress yourself with dark imaginings. Many fears are born of fatigue and loneliness.

Beyond a wholesome discipline, be gentle with yourself. You are a child of the universe no less than the trees and the stars; you have a right to be here.

And whether or not it is clear to you, no doubt the universe is unfolding as it should. Therefore be at peace with God, whatever you conceive Him to be.

> And whatever your labors and aspirations, in the noisy confusion of life, keep peace in your soul. With all its sham, drudgery and broken dreams, it is still a beautiful world. Be cheerful. Strive to be happy.
>
> —Max Ehrmann ©1927

Kill the thing that's killing you.

Life can be pretty f'n epic if you just keep going.

It's crazy that when you think your life is over, it's actually just beginning.

TIMELINE OF OUTTAKES

11/29/1974 | The Birth of Benjamin Robert Mollin
I was born in Blue Island, Illinois, at 5:34 p.m. on a Friday, the firstborn son of Gaetana Lynn Calabrese and James Edward Mollin. When I was brought home, it was baby me, my mom and dad, and my grandpa and grandma Guy and Elinor Calabrese (my grandma's maiden name was Blomberg). We lived in an apartment in Dolton, Illinois. (The current Pope, Leo XIV, is from Dolton. Just sayin'.) Based on old footage of me from my early years at birthday parties and family shit, I seemed a pretty happy little guy. There was no shortage of love.

1978 | Hammond, Indiana
My younger brother, Eric, was born. I'm pretty sure this is around the time I started attending Montessori for preschool and kindergarten.

1980 | Calumet City, Illinois
First grade at Hoover West. My teacher's name was Mrs. Falcon. She had a bun/French twist hairdo and was built like a penguin. I was in love with a girl named Tracy Magnuson. She had long hair and it smelled like flowers.

1981 | 2nd Grade

My teacher's name was Mrs. Stella. She had a perm and was not as penguin-like. Tracy was in my class and I would sit behind her and smell her hair. I remember this like it was yesterday. I'm pretty sure this was around the time I was pissing in the corner of my room like a wolf. I also had a stuffed animal seal named Simpson. I always had it on me, and it would be my favorite stuffed animal literally for years. I rubbed all the fur off its head and occasionally would bite the head as hard as I could. I think we did a play that year for Easter. I remember liking being on stage. This was around the time I started listening to music and learning to play the tuba.

1982 | 3rd Grade

Schrum Elementary (3rd–8th). This school was literally in my backyard. My teacher's name was Mrs. Lilly. As I look back, she looked like a cowboy boot of sorts. She had that year-round "tan" thing going on. This was the year kids were starting to bully me for having a dad that stuttered and for my mom's first name being Gay. (She spelled it G-A-E, but third graders in the early 80s didn't give a fuck.) I was called "Ben G-G-G-Gay."

1983 | 4th Grade

My teacher, Mrs. Sainsberry, had a baby mid-year. Then we had a long-time sub named Mrs. Dietrich. Both had perms and both had brown hair, but Mrs. Sainsberry might have had some cap highlights and a lighter brown color. There were a lot of white Midwesterners with Afros in the early 80s. My mom had quite the Jheri curl.

I pushed a classmate down a flight of stairs for calling me Ben G-G-Gay in front of everyone. He didn't get hurt, but from that day forward, people got a little less mean. I was still called "big head," "Jewboy," and "Ben Melon."

Right around this time, I was showing obvious progress with music. At band concerts, I'd do sax solos while doing the Pee-wee Herman dance. Sometimes my grandpa would take me to the barbershop. He was a sports bookie, and I'd watch the old-time barbers cut hair.

1984 | 5th Grade

Can't remember anything except that it was the year of the Olympics, and I have a lot of baseball cards in my basement from that year. School wise, I think this is the year the girls in class watched a movie about periods. The boys went to the gym for 50 minutes while the girls stayed in class. When we came back to the room, the energy was weird. They seemed traumatized and afraid to make eye contact. No clue who the teacher was.

I remember lying to my friends about video games or toys I had at home to get them to come over to play. The bullying grew less and less. I played baseball, basketball, swam, bowled, and went to Hebrew school. Saturdays and Sundays were always bowling and Jewish shit.

This is when I realized that we weren't broke by society's standards, only Jewish standards. Some of the kids from Sunday school would have birthday parties, and they had nice, big-ass houses with pools and sports cars. Both of my parents worked full-time in education, but we lived on the other side of the tracks.

1985–88 | Junior High

Lots of long hot showers. Busted my head open once at a swim birthday party. Played EPCOT Center in marching band. Had my science teacher in 6th grade try to "groom" me. I had friends, family was cool, everyone was healthy, and we were very happy in our own unique way. We always had non-well-behaved dogs. My grandpa almost killed me in front of my friends for spraying him in the dick with the hose. I wore sweatpants constantly.

My hobbies included video games, masturbation, and loosely organized sports. Got into skateboarding for a hot minute there as well. During the summers from first grade on, I went to a day camp called River Oaks. The elderly couple who ran it had a legit Aunt Jemima look-alike housekeeper who rang a bell when it was dinner time. It's the only way I can explain it.

1988 | Freshman Year

This was the year I attempted suicide. The doctors said that in order for me to attend public school, I would have to wear a helmet and be put in a no-contact, special-ed gym class. That news and the uncertainty of longevity fueled the decision to end my life. I bashed my head against the wall in front of my mom and dad until I passed out. I woke up in NICU neurology at Children's Memorial Hospital. Later on that year, after being taught from home by my teachers for a short stint and receiving surgery, I returned to school and began swim team and low-impact sports.

My girlfriend through high school was one year younger and lived in Hegewisch. She was my first everything. Her dad was a severe alcoholic and at times destroyed the inside of the garage with an ax during blackout spells of being wasted. He was a likable dude, though. Everyone was always afraid of him. He was never a dick to me but was not a fan of the Jews and would, at times, say things.

I was starting to become obsessed with MTV and rock-and-roll. My mom busted me jerking off while smoking a cigarette in the dead of winter in the garage. That year was also the year my dick and balls flew out of my Speedo on a band trip to Florida. Fuck, 88 to 89, that was a tough one.

1989 | Sophomore Year

My mom was still my swim team coach and healthy. I did swim team all four years of high school. Dad was teaching music and doing theater stuff (this was his job and life). He and I would play jazz, and I was getting private saxophone lessons. I'm pretty sure this was the last year I did band and started playing rock-and-roll and punk music. I was getting super good at it.

I was on the path to becoming a pro bowler and a saxophone player. I watched MTV a lot—especially *Yo! MTV Raps*, *120 Minutes*, and *Hairbangers Ball.* I was into hip-hop and metal. I really got into playing guitar. I was able to play Metallica songs minus the solos.

This was the year I gave a spiral perm to a classmate, and I think it's also when I started partying. Mainly drinking a few beers here and there and occasionally robbing my parents' liquor cabinet, which was seldom used. I met my buddy Chris Pena, and we became instant brothers.

1990–1991 | Junior Year

I worked at a bowling alley and as a lifeguard and was playing in high school bands. I even fronted the high school rock band and toured all of the grade schools performing "Hard to Handle" by the Black Crowes.

Sometime during high school, my grandma got her breast removed and started wearing a glove for the lymphoma that came with it. If she didn't, her arm would get grotesquely big. Pretty sure this is around the time my mom was having bronchitis and taking prednisone. She was gaining weight and taking tons of medication to balance the side effects.

My OCD was running wild. Every time I would have sex with my girlfriend, I'd mark it on a calendar with the letters PDGNB, which stood for "Please Dear God No Babies." I would also count the quantity of things I owned so I'd know the number. I thought I wanted to be a lawyer or a mechanical engineer. This summer was all about hanging out, camping, smoking weed, tripping, Cypress Hill, and keggers. I started driving, had my own car, and was really finding my groove.

1992 | Senior Year

I got a tattoo, broke up with my girlfriend, played "Smells Like Teen Spirit" at my high school talent show, and started a three-man mosh pit. I loved music and creative writing. Getting tattooed ruled. I loved everything about it. I got inked up once in the kitchen of an outlaw biker and went to Gary, Indiana, to get tattooed by Roy Boy. They had tigers in the basement. My mom found a quarter pound of weed in my T-shirt drawer. After I graduated high school, I packed a few garbage bags with my shit, started beauty school, and never looked back.

1992–1993 | Beauty School

The year I moved out and went to beauty school, I was broke, but I fucking loved living. I was learning how to tattoo, playing in punk bands, and surrounded by awesome people.

1994 | Age 19

I lived full time for a few months at my buddy Quent's parents' house. Same year, I moved into a one-bedroom apartment in Mokena with a hippy named Jake. My girlfriend was a punk rock theater girl. Her mom would binge-drink vodka in the garage. I asked her to marry me, and she said yes after dating for about a year or so. But we broke up.

I hung out at open mic poetry slams and open mics. Drinking on occasion or at parties and starting to smoke weed once in a while. I met a girl named Gina. She lived in Worth and was super cool. Her mom was a biker chick and her mom's boyfriend was a biker. It's hard to remember all the girlfriends' names. I had a few back then but never at the same time. I've never cheated on any girl I've ever been with. Ever. Not my style.

My grandpa died like Elvis, taking a shit. It was *GoodFellas*. At this time, Chris and Alan were my best friends. We all hung out at a coffeehouse in Homewood called the Extreme Bean. It was right behind an all-ages music venue called Off the Alley. Fuck, was it fun there. Such a scene.

Same year I moved out of my one bedroom with Jake, I moved to Joliet in a one bedroom. First apartment had horrible roaches. I had no furniture, just a couch, TV and tray, and a mattress. They gave me another apartment without roaches next. I heard gunshots. Guy next to me was a drug dealer. Woman across the hall was a hooker and the other dude was a pastor who would jam porn. I lost my mind in this apartment and one night had a full mental breakdown.

I was working at a Supercuts and a FuncoLand. I applied at a place called Armando's and got hired. I had a red Firebird. This is when my career started. I had arrived.

1994–96

In my early 20s, I was living like a rock star. I had an apartment right down the street from Armando's. Was playing sax in a ska band called Hot Stove Jimmy and a few other punk bands. A lot of my friends either went away to college or got blue collar jobs in the area. I worked at salons and would often have to quit them in order to play shows. Also played saxophone in a psychedelic band called Gowhead. Great people and great times.

1997

Owned and operated CC Express and hired my buddy Balsie to run it and shampoo. Bought a house in the town I grew up in. Mom's health was getting scary, and my grandma got her other breast removed. My mom and grandma both had medical lift chairs and, at times, IV bags with open ports. First year of CC Express, I was going out partying and drinking quite often. I started getting a beer belly. I was living the dream.

Playing in some original bands but starting to play music and hang out with Ryan DeYoung.

1998

DeYoung and Balsie were my homies. We were roommates and started playing music immediately. Our house was a studio. A band house. It was fucking awesome. Bands practiced there. We bought recording stuff. I was making bank. Was able to pay credit card debt and fund music. Ryan and I had a band, and Balsie and I had our own band. I was playing original music constantly. Smoking a shit ton of weed and drinking on the regular and dipping my toes into drug culture. The Grapevine and Bobby "Slim" James were mostly weeknights, and original gigs were on the weekends.

I hated the salon I owned. One of my friends who worked for me was pregnant and going through tough times with her baby daddy, so she was missing work a lot. My staff said if I didn't fire her that they were gonna walk. I fired her. Then I sold the salon to this narcissistic asshole who worked there. I stuck around for three months before I bounced. Started my journey with Ryan. We were going out seven days a week, and I was making over six figures, mainly all cash. We'd go downtown and spend $500 on food and drinks quite regularly. We were rock stars.

1999–2004

Signed a lease and borrowed $50,000 from a bank with Ryan to open up a record store/hair salon/resale shop called Bossa Nova. Ryan had a band called Winepress. I learned the songs, and they played a reunion show at a venue called Off the Alley. It was the greatest musical experience ever.

The first year we did well, but then Napster and LimeWire came out, and sales plummeted. We weren't able to make new orders and relied on trade-ins. My haircuts kept the place open during tough times. We had in-store shows with huge touring bands. For two years, we'd throw an outside show with multiple bands and stages and thousands of people would come. We were, and in many ways still are, the punk rock mafia.

We had Bossa Nova from 1999 to 2004. The debt we ran up with loans and credit cards was right around $100,000. I almost ended up getting married to someone who hid a coke problem and a girlfriend from me, so I broke up with her.

My mom was having multiple surgeries, and at times, was not mobile. I was even brought into her recovery after surgery for last rites, and I watched her come back from the dead. Her eyes were bulging out and she kept calling my name. That was a close one.

My best friend and roommate, Alan, killed himself after an argument with his girlfriend. This was the first friend I had who died from suicide. I was devastated. I truly loved Alan.

Ryan and I had a band called Wolcott. We were a solid band with a huge following. From '99 to 2004, it was sex, drugs, and rock-n-roll. Balsie and I had a band called River Oaks. I was a full timer with Bobby "Slim" James, and I was playing in a funk/soul tribute band called The Glow. I even played two shows with Smash Mouth as their horn player at the top of their popularity. Wolcott, at one time, was the record breaker for most original rock shows played in one day. We almost got to be a major label band. I look at videos and pictures and, holy shit, we were nuts and so beautiful and full of life.

Drugs were definitely around, always. Lost a few in our circle to overdoses. I was more of a weed, alcohol, and mushrooms kind of guy. Alcohol was the one that was constant. I was, and would be for years, a functioning alcoholic at that point and into my mid-40s. I still enjoy edibles at night and mushrooms. Mushrooms, I honestly believe, unlocked my creativity.

2005

I rented a chair for three months at a salon called Posh. It was across the street from CC Express, my old salon in Homewood. I was dating a chick who was a supermodel to the eyes but nuttier than a PAYDAY. I helped her open up a shop by my house in Lansing. Eventually, I just worked there for a high percentage and helped manage. We dated for a little under two years. At this time, I put a shampoo bowl in my Cal City house.

2006

I was hustling hair. Had random roommates and a pit bull named Bella. I was extremely minimal and at times would have no food in the fridge. Clients would bring me food, or I'd get Jimmy John's, IHOP, etc., and ration it, which ended up being cheaper than grocery shopping.

Even though I was getting by with the bills, the haunting debt of Bossa Nova made it almost impossible to get ahead. From 1989 to 2017, I never attempted suicide nor was I suicidal in any of my thoughts, but I did stupid, dangerous shit with my buddy Chris. Was playing tons of music with original and cover bands.

2007–2018

I feel like I covered all of this in the book, but here's a brief overview ... Made a hip-hop song called "Haircuts in the Summer."

Used it to land me a spot on *Shear Genius*. Became a reality star on Bravo and a celebrity in the hair world.

Moved from Calumet City, IL, to Munster, IN. Opened up salons and became a traveling artist at the same time. Hated every minute of salon ownership. Loved cutting hair but hated relying on other humans for revenue. Loved being onstage and loved the people who attended the shows. However, I didn't like or trust the corporate people who were involved with that side of my life.

I had money but it was all flying out the window for businesses I didn't want. I was trapped. Looked good on social media but hated the professional life I had created. Reached my boiling point in January of 2018 and my reinvention began after I killed everything.

2018 in a Nutshell

January 24, Dominican hair show.

January 27, Cabo with Angie and Marco.

March 31, Facebook farewell.

April 1, planned suicide. Spoke out to Ang. Stayed home. Put phone on Do Not Disturb. Saw a therapist weekly for three sessions.

May 1, went for a walk.

October 3, Dad died after going into hospice care while I was working a hair show in Cleveland. (I was still traveling constantly with Joico.)

Dec 12, quit Joico over Facebook. Unfollowed everything and everyone. Killed myself off on social media.

2019

Signed up for IRONMAN in Quebec. Hosted Ben Mollin Project trainings throughout the US and Canada. Became introverted and stayed home a lot. Saw some hair clients at home and began training for endurance events. Gave my first motivational speech in Seattle. Ran with David Goggins.

2020

Had bookings for speaking and project classes set up. Did a shit-show hair show and a project in Kansas City in February. When I got home, I got sick as fuck. Marco was at Montessori. St. Patrick's Day 2020 is when Covid started. Everything shut down. Salon was closed. World shut down. I got two industrial face masks and some face shields. I asked the landlord for some slack on rent since we couldn't be open. He said he'd knock off $200 for two months, or I could break the lease and get out of it. We got out.

The basement flooded at the house. I didn't have to pay my mortgage. Holy shit, I was terrified. I'm immune compromised, so travel wasn't an option, which killed my career. Started consulting people over FaceTime for money. I gutted the salon down to the studs. It was therapeutic. Felt good to destroy the last brick and mortar of my past life.

The less I made, the less I had to spend. Life got cheaper, and I didn't have to pay taxes that year. Bought a dry flush toilet and turned a shed into a shit shed. Bought a hand pump sink. This way, clients never had to go in the house. Cut hair outside or inside with great ventilation. Sold equipment and restaurant for enough money for a down payment on an RV. Then we hit the road. It was fucking awesome. I coached people from campgrounds. Did kindergarten with Marco on an iPad, me on a MacBook.

I forced myself to learn how to shoot video. All ultras were off and so were hair shows. I did a Zoom hair show and I hated it. My podcast stopped too. I dislike doing things remotely. It loses its depth. We were home or on the road. We got a new driveway. Socialized outside a lot. Marco did indoor/outdoor sports all of 2020. I ran a shit ton and drinking was going down. Still doing edibles and weed. Marco started playing chess. Angie became a licensed sound therapist.

2021

Taught a hair class at America's Beauty Show. Was more curious on what pandemic shows were like. Signed up for a 50 miler and two 50ks. Loved working from home. Quit drinking in July of that year. Great physical shape and mindset. Never thought about the past. Angie rode 100 miles on her bike. Marco had camp and was in first grade. Walked him to school every day and picked him up. No babysitters at all this whole time.

2022

Angie brings up a photo of me and my family in Hawaii when I was little. Few months later, OLAPLEX flies me to Hawaii. Put Mom's and Grandma's ashes in the ocean. Got home and my Instagram was hacked and deleted. My past life was officially over. I had done it. I eliminated my past. I was a new man. Took our RV to Arizona to spend Christmas in Sedona. It was epic. We traveled the whole state. It was a life-changing experience. Started teaching my project in Cincinnati with Meg Gilbert. Ran 100k and first failed attempt at 100 miles and finished a few 50s.

2023–2025

Started pursuing the dream of becoming an author. Met Lori Lynn and started working on *Deconstructed.* Finished three 100-miler ultra marathons and a 131-miler. Spoke at Beauty with a Purposc, a 15-minute motivational kind of thing. Started drinking again. Quit drinking. Questioned everything. Still do. It's just how I'm wired.

The Future

If God grants me the gift of life, I'll never stop exploring what's possible.

ACKNOWLEDGMENTS

I'd like to thank everyone who I've ever had the pleasure of meeting, working with (or on), all the secondary moms I've made along the way, and all my friends and family. Without you, there is no book.

Fuck. Writing this is hard.

A special extra shout-out to …

Angela Avorio for the constant support, unconditional love, and for keeping Marco and me healthy. Without you, none of this would be happening. You are my angel.

Marco Mollin, for being my son. More than anyone else, this book is for you.

Mom & Dad for being the greatest parents on planet Earth.

Lori Lynn, the universe has a way of putting people in your life right when you need them. Respect the whole time. Grueling. Goal was to create the best thing we could, and we did just that. Working with you, I gained a sister.

Dave Schoon for believing in me and seeing something I never thought in a million years I had. Love you, brother.

Joe Chura for writing the foreword and naming a beer after me. Cal City for life.

Jim Sampagnaro for giving me a stage and showing me how to f'n own it.

Bobby "Slim" James for introducing me to me and giving me a soul.

Nicholas Richards for making me famous with the audition video.

Keon Washington for unpacking the project and being my brother.

Kathy Postma for the honest conversations and unconditional love.

Amanda Stump for reading every word and offering suggestions.

Judy James for introducing me to my publisher.

Shanda at Transcendent Publishing for a kickass cover and turning this manuscript into a real book.

Annie Elizabeth for the invaluable insight and Leslie Simmons for the eagle eyes proofreading.

RJ Magee for unpacking *Shear Genius.*

Christi Bushby for capturing my soul on camera.

Cody Piet for being my punk-rock son.

Danny Giorgi for keeping me a musician.

Ryan DeYoung for 30+ years of brotherhood.

Chris Pena for keeping me young, wild, and free.

Last but not least, a special shout-out to all the haters and anyone who's ever doubted me. Thanks for reading the whole damn book.

ABOUT THE AUTHORS

Ben F'n Mollin is a punk-rock, Cali-sober, non-practicing Jew who went from being a celebrity hairdresser to an overweight, functioning alcoholic turned suicide prevention specialist, endurance athlete, and motivational speaker.

As the founder and creator of The Ben Mollin Project, he hosts transformational events and speaks on topics such as the mindset of a warrior and finding your power.

When he found himself almost $100k in debt, he decided he could either file for bankruptcy or become famous. He became famous after his "Haircuts in the Summer" music video audition landed him a leading role on *Shear Genius.*

After living a life most will only dream about, traveling globally as an industry celebrity, the pressures of balancing work and family had turned him into a ticking time bomb.

He hit his breaking point and decided to burn it all down. By 2018, he deconstructed everything, killing his career instead of himself.

In under a year, he lost 65 pounds and completed his first IRONMAN in 2019, becoming unrecognizable to those who had known him. That same year, he ran his first of many ultra marathons, recently finishing a 130-mile race through the trail system of northern Arizona. To date, he has clocked over tens of thousands of miles (and counting).

In 2024, a month before his 50th birthday, he paced a record-breaking 70-year-old ultra marathon runner for the last 53 miles of a 100-mile race in Central Illinois. Six months later, on May 9, 2025, he returned to the Sedona Canyon 125 to finish what he started. What had almost destroyed him at age 49 became one of the most profound spiritual experiences of his life at age 50.

A walking art project, Ben grew up in the south suburbs of Chicago in the city of Calumet City, Illinois, with parents who managed their disabilities and loved without condition.

Ben, his creative-genius wife Angela, and their martial-arts trained, chess-prodigy son Marco, live part-time in Munster, Indiana, and love to travel in their RV.

To connect with Ben and read more of his writing, head over to:

benfnmollin.com

The writer who has laughed and cried her way through capturing Ben's stories for this book is book architect, **Lori Lynn**. She has worked on more than 100 books as an editor or ghostwriter, but this is her first credit as a co-author.

Born in New Jersey and raised in Kentucky, Lori and her three children now live in Nashville, TN. She grew up with one sister but no brothers. Ben has become the brother she never knew she needed.

She brought the tattoo ratio way down among Ben's publishing team, but as soon as her trio of kids become legal adults (which happens in 2028), Judah, Mira, and Dia have promised to get matching dragonfly tattoos.

She hopes you enjoy *DECONSTRUCTED: Kill the Thing That's Killing You* so much that you recommend it to your friends and family and leave an online review!

Connect with Lori at: **LoriLynnOnline.com**

YOUR NEW F'N MANTRA

One of the things that helped to get me out of my funk was looking at myself in the mirror every day and saying these words out loud:

I am beautiful. I am fearless. I am strong.

Now, whenever I'm asked to speak, or I'm hosting one of my projects, I have everyone get out their phones, turn on the video camera, and record themselves saying it. We gradually increase in volume from a level 5 to a level 10. By level 10, we're shouting at the top of our lungs.

Every day for the next 21 days (three weeks), I challenge you to get in front of a mirror or use your phone camera, look yourself in the eyes, and say:

I am beautiful. I am fearless. I am strong.

Share your experience publicly online with the hashtags #thebenmollinproject and #screamit or privately by going to:

BENFNMOLLIN.COM

www.ingramcontent.com/pod-product-compliance
Lightning Source LLC
Chambersburg PA
CBHW060415130626
46555CB00005B/2079
9798999203014